Contents

List of Illustrations

The Session Man.

To Belinda and to Susan

The *Session* Man.

The story of "Bobby Graham"
the uk's greatest session drummer.

Patrick Harrington and Bobby Graham

BROOM
HOUSE

First published in Great Britain by
Broom House Publishing Limited,
Broom House, Raglan,
Monmouthshire, NP15 2HW.

© Bobby Graham
and Patrick Harrington 2004.

ISBN 0-9549142-0-1
A CIP record for this title is available
from the British Library.

All photographs are from
Bobby Graham's collection
The quotations from Ray Davies and
Dave Davies from *X Ray* and *Kink*
respectively are with their permission.

Printed and bound in Great Britain
by CPD Wales, Ebbw Vale.

Preface

During the course of writing this book one question has been asked repeatedly. How did I get involved?

I was travelling home a year or so ago when I heard Bobby Graham being interviewed on the radio. The interview was on Radio Wales and was conducted by Mal Pope who is, himself, an accomplished musician and singer/songwriter. It was a very good interview. I found it fascinating. When I got home I looked up Bobby Graham's website. After reading its contents, I sent an email to Bobby Graham saying how much I had enjoyed the interview and telling him how much I appreciated the contribution he made to sixties music. He telephoned me and we had a long chat. I asked Bobby whether he had thought of writing a book about his experiences. This was a mistake on my part because within minutes I had volunteered to help.

Bobby Graham has provided a great deal of factual information about himself and others. I have spoken to many people, some of whom are quoted in the book. I have conducted such research as it is possible to do.

It became clear early on that it was not going to be possible to set things out in a strict chronological order. The exigencies of the music industry and the passage of time simply do not permit this. There are bound to be mistakes; none are intentional. Memories have faded. Records of recording session were few. The pace of Bobby Graham's life was fast and furious.

For all his undoubted musical achievements Bobby Graham is a modest man. He does not boast about what he has done. I took the unilateral decision that the book should be written in the third person. It makes it easier to tell the truth about an amazingly talented man and what Bobby Graham did during this most intriguing musical period.

I have enjoyed writing this book. I hope you enjoy reading it.

Patrick Harrington
Raglan, October 2004

Introduction

By the time that he became a session man, Bobby Graham already had an established musical pedigree. He had been the drummer with The Outlaws, who were Joe Meek's house band. With Joe Meek he had played on some of the defining songs of the time. He left The Outlaws to join Joe Brown and The Bruvvers with whom he toured and recorded extensively. After The Bruvvers he joined Marty Wilde's Wildcats and toured, played and recorded with him. He then played with, and effectively ran, The John Barry Seven.

His talents and precision drumming were spotted by record producers; he was enticed into session work. He became one of a small number of session musicians whose services were in huge demand at a time when the British pop music industry was taking the world by storm. The part that this dedicated band of session musicians played in our pop music heritage cannot be overstated. Bobby called them "The Musical Stuntmen." Without them the soundtrack of the sixties would have been very different.

In a ten year period Bobby Graham played on over fifteen thousand tracks. Records on which he played spent over two hundred weeks in the top ten. Throughout the time, the contribution that he and almost all other session players made was unacknowledged by the front line artists with whom they played. It was kept secret by the record companies and was largely unknown to the public who bought the records. The contribution the session men made is truly enormous. They were a very talented group of musicians.

Bobby Graham's is an extraordinary story. Here it is.

The Early Years

Bobby Graham was born Robert Francis Neate on the 11th of March 1940. His home was in Edmonton, North London. He was the first son of Robert and Elsie Neate. His father worked as a GPO telephone engineer whilst his mother was a housewife. Bobby remembers it as an ordinary, happy childhood. He was never very close to either parent and describes his father as being a kind and humane man but with a streak of Victorian discipline. The family was complete when Bobby's brother Ian was born.

The family was not musical, in the sense that neither parent sang nor played a musical instrument; they did, though, own a wind-up gramophone and a limited collection of, mostly pre-war, 78s. It wasn't played much by Bobby's parents and so when Bobby's musical interests began to develop it was he who became its principal user.

Much has been written on the contentious subject of whether musicians are born or made. Whilst the influence of teaching, dedication and determination cannot be over valued, it seems commonly to be accepted that some have a greater innate talent than others. Many believe that such a talent often surfaces even in the absence of direct stimulus. So it seems to have been in this case.

Bobby Graham (as he was to become) has a clear recollection of how it was that his father came to make him his first drum kit and by so doing set him on the course that he took. Bobby had developed the habit of tapping his dinner plate with knife and fork. After a second consecutive day of breaking a plate, his father, with a mixture of anger, exasperation and prescience said: "can you please stop breaking the plates" although followed it quickly by saying: "I'd better build you a drum kit." And so he did. He was a clever and dextrous man, well used to the art of improvisation after the privations of war. Within a few days he had completed his task.

Bobby was seven years of age and was delighted with the kit his father made. Several, differently sized, round biscuit tins had heavy rubber sheeting stretched over them which was glued and fixed to the sides of each tin. Drumsticks were made from cut down pieces of dowelling. For Bobby it was enough to practice on and practice he did.

Little Bobby Neate was an introverted child; he did not excel at anything at school and had no interest in playing or watching sport. His bright ginger hair set him apart from most of his peers and he did not make friends easily. However, in his own bedroom he was in a different world, a world of his own: playing to enthusiastic audiences whose rapturous applause drove him to practice even more avidly. This was many years before the television age and Bobby often wonders where he drew this inspiration from.

It took his parents less than three months to understand that this was not a passing fad. They realised that Bobby had found something he really enjoyed. They were not to know that it was also something at which he could excel but the parental instinct seems to have been fairly finely honed. As the result of a gigantic leap of faith they decided that Bobby was to be encouraged in what was already his abiding passion. As he approached his eighth birthday they determined that he should have a proper drum kit as his birthday present.

Bobby remembers well the day that he acquired his first kit. His father had read a newspaper advertisement for Ted Warren's Drum Shop and took his son there one Saturday morning. The shop was in Bow, East London and was a genuine emporium. As little Bobby went inside he entered a state of Nirvana. Ted Warren would, no doubt, have been proud if he had known that this little ginger haired customer would later be acknowledged as the greatest British session drummer ever. As it was the customer was served with enthusiasm and an entirely appropriate beginner's kit.

Objectively, his first 'real' drum kit was a modest affair but to Bobby it was beyond his wildest dreams. A second hand snare drum was matched with a bass drum and bass drum-mounted tom-toms and a single small ride cymbal. A pair of wire brushes, were included at Ted Warren's insistence "all good drummers have them" although their new owner had no idea what they were or what to do with them. The kit had no floor tom-tom, no hi-hat, no array of cymbals but it still had everything that Bobby needed. Looking back after almost sixty years of drumming, Bobby remains firmly of the view that, "it was the greatest drum kit ever."

The kit was set up in his bedroom and Bobby practised and practised and practised.

Post-war austerity was abating and making way for the acquisitive society which Britain became. Resources which had been channelled into the war effort were now creating a profusion of electrical products. So it was that the next significant purchase in the Neate household was a record player. By modern standards, or even those of a decade later, it was a primitive device; it was though plenty to further Bobby's practice regime. It was not long before his parents were persuaded to let Bobby 'borrow' the player for his bedroom. There, he played the 78s of Bing Crosby, The Andrews Sisters and The Glenn Miller Orchestra. He played along with the drumbeat and within a short time he felt able to mimic every beat. Although not many years later his practice method became more sophisticated it was these early practice sessions which instilled the standards which Bobby set and to which others could only aspire. Later, with the acquisition of a three-speed player he was able to slow the tracks to 33rpm; this allowed him the better to isolate the drum play and hear the nuances and stylistic subtleties.

Bobby was not living in musical isolation because a close, though much older, neighbour was already an accomplished guitarist. The Neates' landlord lived two doors away. The son of the family was called Gerald Hart. He was probably about twenty when Bobby first heard him play. He was very good. When Bobby learned that Gerald played in a band, he became Bobby's idol. Interestingly, in those days, they were called 'bands'. Ten years later they were called 'groups' but still later the nomenclature reverted to the original and they became bands again.

Bobby's musical education advanced as the result of Gerald Hart's benign and tolerant attitude. He allowed Bobby to hear him play even when he was trying new numbers. It was not just the music that enthralled Bobby, it was the fact Gerald shared his knowledge of the music industry. He had an early multi-track tape recorder and laid down guitar tracks in a fashion Bobby had never known about. This was the very early fifties so Gerald Hart was quite a trendsetter.

When Bobby was twelve years of age Gerald called one Saturday and asked Bobby's parents a favour. He explained that his band was booked to play at a local wedding that evening but the band's drummer had let them down. He went on to explain that they could not play without a drummer and asked permission for Bobby to be allowed to fill in. Although they were concerned at his youth, Bobby was allowed to play. He still remembers the excitement of the evening. The band's repertoire comprised quick steps, fox trots and waltzes. Bobby's incessant practice paid its first dividends and the band members were happy with his playing; this was the more remarkable because he had never even practised with them before.

Another person who had a profound influence upon the growing Robert Neate was a market stallholder who was known as Toffee Apple Mac – a soubriquet which derived from his former market wares. By the time that he entered Bobby's world, he was selling records at the open air market held at Edmonton Green each Saturday. Bobby began to help out on the stall. His payment was the opportunity to listen to music all day and become familiar with the latest artistes.

The musical world was rapidly changing and the new sounds emanated from Frankie Laine, Johnnie Ray, Doris Day and Rosemary Clooney. Frankie Laine was a major star in the pre rock'n'roll era, spending an unequalled 27 weeks at the top of the charts in 1953 and at one time had three singles in the top five. Even today when Bobby hears Frankie Laine's 'I Believe' he is transported back to Edmonton Green and Toffee Apple Mac. This Saturday 'work' was part of Bobby's hobby and he relished the prospect of being surrounded by the profound musical influences of the day.

Summer holidays for the Neate family were always taken at Canvey Island. Distances were apparently different in those days and to young Bobby Canvey Island seemed a long way away. But the journey was worth it because once he was there he found that it was full of exciting things; it is also where Bobby made his first recording. On the sea front there was a small recording booth where members of the public could record straight onto a 7-inch wax disc. After walking past it several times Bobby finally plucked up the courage to go in. He said that he wanted to make a record. He was asked what he would like to sing. With no vocal ambitions, Bobby said that he was a drummer. There was no drum kit so this presented a bit of a problem. However, his enthusiasm was obvious, became contagious and a 'kit' was improvised. So Bobby Neate recorded 'Cherry Pink and Apple Blossom White' playing a metal chair with two screwdrivers. He was accompanied by the engineer's assistant on piano. Bobby was very proud of his first recording but sadly the disc has not survived.

Back at home Bobby's musical interests widened and he became interested in jazz. Of those then playing Bobby had a special admiration for The Stan Kenton Orchestra. They had had a major success with a number called 'Peanut Vendor' a Latin piece with an intriguing drum part. Bobby bought the record and played along with it until he was master of every beat. From then on, he bought every Stan Kenton record and his lifelong love of jazz was born.

This was not the only change in Bobby's life. He, together with millions of others, had become 'teenagers' a word and concept which crossed the Atlantic in the early years of the 1950s. This was not the only trans-atlantic import. Bobby also became aware of the new musical phenomenon which had derived from the same source; rock'n'roll. It would be easy to write that Bobby was immediately captivated and an instant convert but this would be a distortion of the truth. His, and almost everyone else's, first recollection of this new musical genre was hearing 'Rock Around The Clock' by Bill Haley and The Comets which had caused a sensation. The truth is that Bobby still bought more jazz records than any other musical format; his musical taste also embraced the new sounds and he particularly enjoyed the music of Tennessee Ernie Ford, who enjoyed UK chart success in the mid-fifties. Of his songs Bobby particularly liked 'Shotgun Boogie' which although not a hit in the UK was well-received. He also recalls the impact that Merrill Moore made with 'House of Blue Lights'.

By playing along with these Bobby widened his reper-toire and learned the rudiments of rock'n'roll drumming. In retrospect, he realises how fortunate he was not to have been merely a follower of fashion.

It was only a few years later that Bobby Graham's talent attracted many admirers; it was not just his skill but also his versatility. The hundreds of hours spent closeted away in his bedroom paid great dividends but, as later events will disclose, these dividends did not come free.

By the time he reached the age of fifteen, Bobby's personality was formed. Although it was many years before the clinical diagnosis was made, Bobby had developed an obsessive compulsive disorder or 'obsessive personality'. His dedication to practice was one manifestation. Sadly, there was to be a darker side and the success that followed came at a price. A very high price.

The Real World

Robert Neate left school at fifteen with no formal qualifications. He lacked the self-confidence to seek a musical career although it is what he would dearly have loved to have done. His introversion drove him to seek a job that, he felt, suited his personality although this may have been done subconsciously. He became a Trainee Projectionist at the Regal Cinema in Edmonton.

It was an ideal job for Bobby. It was 1955 and still the age of the cinema. Relatively few people had television sets and those that did had a 'choice' of one channel, the BBC. Programmes were broadcast in black & white for five hours in the evening. 'Daytime TV' was limited to an afternoon Children's Hour. To today's Sky generation, television then would appear almost prehistoric, screens often measuring a mere twelve inches across the diagonal. In contrast, the cinema showed films, often in glorious Technicolor, which transported the audience to a different world.

At the Regal it was not just the audiences that were held in thrall. The Trainee Projectionist also loved it. Bobby remembers his favourite films, although of course the direction his life has taken may put a Technicolor gloss on his recollection: "I loved *The Gene Krupa Story* starring Sal Mineo and *The Benny Goodman Story* starring Steve Allen. Then of course there was *The Glenn Miller Story*."

This was not an age of a film showing for a week and then appearing on video a few months later. Popular films were often repeated, sometimes as matinées. Bobby Neate was always willing to play the matinées when he could watch such films. It was probably watching Gene

Krupa playing his 'drumnastics' that persuaded Bobby that the lure of the stage and drumming professionally may be a realistic ambition after all.

These fertile thoughts were greatly enhanced by the Sunday Evening concerts held at the Regal. During this period cinemas did not play films on Sundays and so they were often used for other forms of entertainment. The Regal had a large auditorium, seating eleven hundred people, so it was a suitable venue for even the most popular attractions. Bobby could not believe his good fortune when he was asked to work one Sunday and he discovered that The Stan Kenton Orchestra was to play. Bobby remembers it well: "They were brilliant. It was as though they had read my mind and played everything I loved. I couldn't wait to get back to my kit." Lots of other top orchestras and bands played the Regal – and Bobby saw them all – Lionel Hampton, Jack Parnell, The Ted Heath Orchestra and many others. The highlights for Bobby were the double drum duets played by Jack Parnell and Phil Seaman; numbers like 'Skin Deep' and 'The Hawk Talks' had an enduring effect upon him.

The real thrill came when he saw the great Ronnie Verrall play with The Ted Heath Orchestra. Ronnie Verrall was regarded as 'the drummers' drummer'. His technical proficiency and his ability to improvise made him a legend. Ronnie Verrall had already been a major influence on Bobby, ever since he first heard him play on records. To stand in the wings watching him was a treat.

Unfortunately, Bobby was a gauche teenager; he lacked the confidence to make any attempt to speak to Ronnie Verrall, even just to ask for an autograph. Fortunately, time and fate intervened and it was not many years before they met. When they did meet they became professional colleagues and close friends; after much prodding, Bobby accepts that they also became mutual admirers: "It was great. I had grown up thinking he was the best. I still think he was the best. But for him to say "well done, I like that" was worth more than anything. We played a lot on the session circuit and I know that he was always kind about me as well as to me."

The catalogue of other artists that came to the Regal is an extensive one. A sign of the times came when hundreds of people slept outside the Regal just to be sure of getting tickets for a concert: to watch Bill Haley and The Comets. Rock'n'roll had arrived in Edmonton. The concert provided a visual display of the teddy boy culture which was then an epidemic. Although it added to the excitement of the evening, it attracted much authority and parental disapprobation.

As previously indicated 'Rock Around the Clock' was the first rock'n'roll record that Bobby remembers hearing. The story of the song and the singer fits well into the narrative of session musicians. Bill Haley had been a journeyman musician for some years before making this recording. He had not made a success of being a singing cowboy and his attempts at being a radio station impresario had met with only limited approval. His band, Billy Haley and his Saddlemen, was renamed after Bob Johnson, a radio station director of programmes, made a cute astronomical suggestion that "Bill Haley should have a band called The Comets". He had made the charts with 'Rock The Joint' and 'Crazy Man Crazy' in 1953. On the 12th of April 1954, armed with a new recording contract, he went to the Pythian Temple Studio in New York to record 'Thirteen Women (and Only One Man in Town)'. The B side was to be a song he had been playing at gigs for over a year. B sides counted for little. It was pared to basics musically and recorded in two takes with the engineers splicing the second part of the second take onto the first part of the first take.

Musically, the defining sounds were the rim shots of Billy Gussak and the guitar break of Danny Cedrone. This riff had been know as 'Cedrone's solo' for some time; he had played it on Bill Haley's 'Rock the Joint' so it was not even original. The A side sold the press run of 75,000 and would have disappeared but for a quirk of fate. One of the writers of 'Rock Around The Clock', Jim Myers touted it around the Film Studios and it was chosen by Pandro S. Berman to play over the credits of the new Glenn Ford film *The Blackboard Jungle*. The film identified with the new teenage generation and their angst. When the movie was released in America in March 1955 'Rock around the Clock' was already Number 1 there. It had briefly reached the lower reaches of the UK charts but then re-entered coincidentally with the film's release in the UK in October 1955. This time it got to Number 1 and stayed in the charts for seventeen weeks. It re-entered the charts six times over the next twenty years and will always be remembered as the song which launched rock'n'roll. What is the relevance of all of this to our story? Billy Gussak and Danny Cedrone were session players who were paid a single fee for playing on the record – twenty-one dollars each.

Many other American acts played at the Regal. Guy Mitchell had the girls swooning; Frankie Lymon and The Teenagers proved to be a very popular live act and the big bands and orchestras continued to fill the seats.

Bobby is sure that the diversity of these musical experiences had a profound effect upon his playing. "The one thing they all had was a drummer. I would stand in the wings, often on a level with the vocalist but always with a perfect view of the drummer. On consecutive weeks I might see a 52 piece orchestra, a five piece rock'n'roll outfit and then a 12 piece band. I always watched the drummer. Some were very good and inspirational but, the funny thing is, I think the bad ones probably inspired me more because I knew I could do that or maybe better."

Another musical influence that emerged at this time was skiffle. The attractions of skiffle were many. To the listener it was a new and exciting sound. To the aspiring player, it was the apparent simplicity of the music coupled with the accessibility of the 'instruments.' In many skiffle groups a tea chest with broom-handle bass and a washboard played with thimbles were the rhythm section, providing accompaniment to a guitar and banjo.

One of the usherettes at the Regal had a son who had started his own skiffle group. She mentioned to Bobby that her son was looking for somebody to play washboard. In a rare gesture of one-upmanship, Bobby was able to tell her that he could play drums and had his own drum kit. He was invited to join and them and happily did. He found that this new ensemble had their own string bass player. They were a very superior outfit. They were called The Hangmen.

Things went well. They practised hard and were soon very popular in the village halls. They covered most of the skiffle tunes of the day, including those played by Les Hobeuxs and The Charles McDevitt Skiffle Group featuring Shirley Whiskey who had a massive hit with 'Freight Train' in 1957. Of course, they also played the songs of the great Lonnie Donegan, the King of Skiffle, whose hits had begun in January the previous year. Lonnie Donegan is acknowledged by many as being the most influential UK recording artist before The Beatles. He had twenty-eight consecutive top thirty chart entries and was the first UK male artist to score two top ten hits in America.

Bobby's esteem rose when his group was asked to play at the Christmas Party for the staff at the Regal. This was almost certainly Christmas 1956. The gig was a great success. Playing skiffle served to expand Bobby's musical horizons. He got to hear other types of music and meet other musicians, among them the talented trumpet-player, Mike Brown. By the time they met, Mike Brown was ensconced in a jazz band which played each Sunday at a smoke-filled, dimly-lit basement in Hampstead called The Witches Cauldron. Bobby was invited to sit in. He rapidly established himself as the resident drummer. This was real jazz in a real jazz environment. Bobby discovered that jazz players lived a pretty bohemian life. It intrigued him and attracted him. He soon discovered that most of the musicians had changed their names; this was not just a trend with front line singers but with musicians too. So, after a rare episode of domestic disharmony, Bobby stuck a pin in a telephone directory and adopted the surname the pin chose. He has been 'Bobby Graham' ever since.

As mentioned previously, Bobby played 78s at 33rpm to learn the drum parts. He struggled with only one, Louis Bellson playing 'Skin Deep' with The Duke Ellington Orchestra. Bobby spent months trying to play the bass drum as fast as Louis Bellson but never quite managed it. "It was years later I learned that Louis Bellson had two bass drums and was playing with both feet. No wonder I couldn't do it. Still it was good practice."

Bobby was by now an avid collector of the new format LPs and EPs. His taste was eclectic, predominantly jazz but with the occasional rock'n'roll. He became familiar with the work of Gene Krupa playing with The Benny Goodman Orchestra. He discovered The Dave Brubeck Quartet with the wonderful drumming of Joe Morello. Above all else and all others it was the playing of Buddy Rich that captivated Bobby. He first heard this on an album called *Norman Granz Presents Jazz At The Philharmonic*. "Buddy Rich was the simply the best drummer ever. His playing was almost abnormal, so fast. No-one has ever been able to emulate the roaring technique. I saw him many times later on when he was playing with his own band. Quite simply, he was a phenomenon."

Jazz was Bobby's first love: a friend, Chas Hodges, described him as a 'jazz snob'. However, his taste was secretly becoming increasingly diverse. He gradually began to buy more and more rock'n'roll records, although he was careful to conceal them if his jazz friends came to call.

Although music was the dominant influence in

Bobby's life, as it had been for ten years, something then happened to promote it still further. One day early in 1960 there was a ring on the doorbell at his home at 28 Church Street. It was to change his life for ever. Welcome to the world of rock'n'roll.

The Stormers: Butlins, Birds and Booze

One February day in 1960, Bobby opened the front door of his parents' house. Standing on the doorstep was an old friend of his, a talented singer named Billy Gray. Billy Gray's real surname was Halsey but some time before he had reached the conclusion that this did not sound like the sort of name a rock star would have, so he had adopted a different moniker. Billy had made quite a name for himself locally, fronting a group called Billy Gray and The Stormers. He was ambitious and looking to expand the group's geographical experience. The purpose of his visit was to recruit Bobby Graham as their drummer. Billy Gray had a specific project in mind. He had arranged to audition for a summer season at Butlins Holiday Camps. He was confident that this would set Billy Gray and The Stormers on the road to fame and fortune.

Bobby listened to the proposal as outlined by Billy Gray. He was not interested. He did not wish to prostitute himself with a constant diet of rock'n'roll. He was a purist; jazz was his love. The interview was not going well for Billy Gray so he played his trump card: "It's twenty pounds a week – each: all meals and accommodation are included and there will be loads of birds."

Twenty pounds a week! Bobby swiftly sold his soul to the devil and signed up. There followed a frenetic period of rehearsal and acclimatisation to the group's repertoire. The other members of the band were Billy Kuy, the dapper lead guitarist, always immaculately attired in a stiff white collar and tie with highly burnished shoes. The rhythm guitarist was Reg Hawkins, who was always ready for a laugh. The bass guitarist was a very talented sixteen year old whose sartorial style was the antithesis of that of Billy Kuy: his name was Chas Hodges, who later found fame as half of the irrepressible duo Chas'n'Dave. He remains a close friend of Bobby Graham. Bobby recollects that Chas was a typical sixteen year old. He slept a lot and did not dress to impress. Billy Kuy remembers their first rehearsal: "I knew of Bobby before we met because we had all discussed asking him to join us. He was a couple of years older than the rest of us and we knew he could play the drums. My first impression was not that favourable. He could certainly play, a lot better than the rest of us but he seemed a bit arrogant as though he was demeaning himself playing this rubbish."

Interestingly, Billy Kuy was and remains firmly of the view that Bobby Graham had had formal training and was able to read music. In neither respect is he right but it tends to show that ability creates its own aura.

The group played a number of gigs locally before the audition. They had a Friday night residency at The Kings Head at Edmonton Green. This is memorable to Bobby because it was here that he discovered for the first time that he liked the effect that alcohol had upon him. He had never before enjoyed drinking; he realised that a couple of drinks turned him from a shy introvert into a relaxed extrovert. He felt more confident with his playing and it soon became his habit to drink before playing.

The Butlins' audition was held at the Majestic Ballroom, Finsbury Park. There was stiff competition for a limited number of places but Billy Gray and The Stormers were slick and professional and were offered the job; it was to be a Summer Season at the Filey holiday camp in Yorkshire.

The Butlins holiday camp concept was a phenomenon. In the decades before package holidays to the continent, the enterprising Billy Butlin had recognised the opportunity that cheap catered holidays could provide for the mass market. He had taken leases on a number of unused army barracks and turned them into holiday camps. The billets became 'chalets' with adequate if Spartan furnishing and three meals per day were included in the cost. A rich and varied diet of entertainment was essential to the formula. The camps were run with almost military discipline and with a futile moral ethos which did not recognise that the majority of campers came on holiday in search of romance. The Filey camp was the biggest Butlins and it was a long way from London.

Bobby Graham and Chas Hodges travelled to Filey in Bobby's Austin A40 pick up, with an improvised tent covering all of the band's equipment in the back.

On arrival their first impression was that they had stepped onto the set of a World War 2 film. When they were allocated their chalets Bobby remembers that the most prominent feature were the Regulations displayed on the wall. No visitors of the opposite sex were allowed in the chalet, drink in moderation only, the chalets were to be kept clean and tidy: all of this was calculated to test the behaviour of a group of musicians enjoying their first taste of freedom, far away from home.

The group performed in the Rock and Calypso Ballroom. They played covers of Cliff Richard and the Shadows, The Everly Brothers, Roy Orbison and lots more. They were quick to learn the latest hits and their repertoire increased weekly. Their set was constantly modified to meet the demands of the audience. The ballroom had a capacity of between four and five hundred and was packed every night they played. It was very hard work but, at first, it didn't seem like work.

Another novelty that they came thoroughly to enjoy was that they were expected to provide backing for guest singers. This sometimes proved an interesting challenge; often the visiting singer would perform a number familiar to The Stormers but in a different key than they were used to playing. This did not trouble the drummer who often found amusement in his colleagues discomfiture.

Billy Gray had been right about the money, right about the accommodation and right about the food. He was also right about the 'birds'. The 'campers' were at the camp for one week or two, never more. They left their inhibitions behind when they packed for their annual treat. There was time to meet, become close and profess undying affection before a tearful parting and promises to write. As one group of campers left on a coach for the railway station the camp was made ready for the next holiday makers who arrived on the same coaches having been collected from the station. It was, says Bobby, a very happy time. "I went from having no girl on my arm to having a different one each week or, more often, each time we played. It was the beginning of the swinging sixties and we all entered into the spirit of it."

There was also a more formal band with a residency at Butlins; they played in the Gaiety Theatre. It was The Teddy Foster Orchestra of whom Bobby had long been an admirer. The music they played was to the conventional dance audience, the tunes of Glenn Miller being particular favourites. They were mostly jazz players and the band eschewed rock'n'roll. The drummer was named Johnnie Sawyer and, says Bobby, he was very good. He and Bobby got on very well together and became firm friends. They suggested to Teddy Foster that they play a drum duet. The bandleader was unenthusiastic seeing Bobby as a member of some lesser species, a rock'n'roll drummer, therefore, necessarily, bereft of talent. He was, though, gracious enough to suggest that they could try it at rehearsal.

Bobby and Johnnie devised a duet based on 'Skin Deep' the drum classic written by Louis Bellson, something that Bobby had practised many times. They were also influenced by the famous Gene Krupa/ Buddy Rich battle of the drums duet played at New York's Carnegie Hall in 1952.

Teddy Foster had not previously heard Bobby play; he

was absolutely delighted. From questioning the concept he became a great enthusiast. This then became a regular feature; on one night a week the orchestra played as The Teddy Foster Band and Bobby would join them for the drum duet. This was Bobby's first experience of playing with a big band. The feature was introduced as a 'battle of the drums' and proved not only to be great fun but immensely popular and greatly appreciated.

The vocalist with the band seemed always to enjoy it and led the applause. She was a talented singer, known then as Julie Rolls; she enjoyed great success later in the sixties as Julie Rogers. Her recording of 'The Wedding' was a massive hit, reaching Number 3 in the charts and remaining in the top twenty for almost six months. Billy Kuy was also very impressed with this item. "It was spectacular. You would swear that they must have played together for years, not days. I could tell then, if I didn't know it already, that Bob Graham was going to make a name for himself."

However, fun though it all was, the novelty soon began to wear off. The food, whilst plentiful, was boring and repetitive. The constant announcements over the tannoy became a source of irritation and sharing two to a chalet for months tested the comradeship of the group's members. "Before we were half-way through the residency we were all screaming to get back home," relates Billy Kuy. "The monotony had got to us and although we all got on well enough, little things began to grate. To be honest, Bobby and I were never particular friends, then or later and I think we all used to get on each others' nerves. Bobby was particularly unimpressed with a practical joke we played on him. One night two members of the group 'borrowed' a searchlight bulb from one of the fittings on the Stalag. Bobby was having an early night in his chalet when all of sudden he was woken by this 1,000 watt bulb that had been fitted to the light fitting just above his head."

So it is unsurprising that Bobby found the shared

chalet to be claustrophobic. This, coupled with his burgeoning friendship with members of The Teddy Foster
Orchestra, led him to seek alternative accommodation at
the Reighton Hall Country Club, where he rented an attic
room. He spent his nights after the residency playing jazz
and drinking at Reighton Hall. The regime of no girls in
the rooms was replicated in this establishment, run by a
man named Derek Jessop and his formidable mother. As
with Butlins this merely created a challenge to be over-
come, and it frequently was. Moving out and allying
himself with members of 'the opposition' as others may
have perceived it, had the effect of isolating Bobby from
the other members of The Stormers.

On the whole, however, they were happy days and
Bobby loved the musical experiences that Filey presented.
But the dark clouds were gathering and he was beginning
to succumb. He spent his Thursdays at Scarborough,
alone, but with the company of a half bottle of whisky. It
was not for some time that he realised it, but Bobby was
rapidly descending into a state of alcoholism. It was a different Bobby Graham that ended the season at Filey to the
one that started there only four months before.

Suddenly, the season ended. The coaches took the
campers to the railway station but did not return. So it
was back to London to see what fate held in store for Billy
Gray and The Stormers.

Disappointing days but then we became Outlaws

The return to London proved to be very depressing. After months of playing daily to enthusiastic audiences, they found a great void in their musical lives. Worse, there proved to be little work for the group. Before they had left for Filey they had been busy, with a Friday night residency and the offer of lots of other gigs. They came back to discover that they seemed scarcely to have been missed, there were very few gigs, they had no manager or agent and they had no direction, musical or otherwise.

The horrible thought struck them individually and as a group that they may have to get 'proper' jobs. So they did. Billy Gray left them hoping to further his career as a soloist. Chas left to work in a factory producing deckchairs. Billy Kuy joined him and managed a morning shift before deciding that the work was not for him. Reg Hawkins, alone, made a success of his career move, joining an Optical Company where he worked happily until his retirement.

Bobby tried to retain his musical links and did so to the extent that he joined the firm of Firth Brothers who had a piano shop on the Broadway in Edmonton. The premises were impressive but the job less so. Bobby's principal function was delivering pianos. He describes the atmosphere as redolent of 'Grace Brothers' a decade or so later. Messrs Firth were each addressed as 'Mr Firth' until the employee had been in service long enough to address them as 'Mr Raymond' or 'Mr David'. Bobby never reached such exalted status. He left, feeling that he was at risk of expiring with boredom. His recollection is incomplete as to whether he chose to leave or he left with no choice. In either event, they were not happy days.

One of the up-and-coming visiting singers that The Stormers had backed at Filey was a man named Danny Rivers. By the time The Stormers returned to London they found that Danny was making quite a name for himself. He had already appeared on some of legendary Jack Good's seminal television shows – *The Six Five Special* on the BBC and later on *Oh Boy* on the commercial channel.

At Butlins opportunities for the visiting singer and the group to rehearse before the show were strictly limited. Sometimes the guest would arrive too late to rehearse at all. It tended not to matter too much if the singer was seeking only to replicate the popular songs of the day; a problem could arise if the singer's repertoire included numbers unfamiliar to the group. Billy Kuy explains: "Historically bands booked for a season's residency had been able to sight read music but that had all changed with rock'n'roll. None of the guitarists in The Stormers could read although I always thought that Bobby could. Fortunately, the singers couldn't read either so if they asked us to play something we didn't know we either said "no" or he would have to take his chances."

Danny Rivers' appearance at Filey had gone particularly well and the group had been tight and cohesive. Danny Rivers' manager had been impressed. He was an interesting man named Peter Jacwinandi.

So it was that, after the summer season had ended, and The Stormers, although theoretically extant, were 'resting,' a call from 'Jac' was received and was very welcome. He had heard that Billy Gray had left the band. He phoned Bobby Graham and asked if he would be interested in re-forming The Stormers to back a new singer that Jac was also managing. The singer was now named Mike Berry. He, too, had been encouraged to change his surname from his birth name of Bourne.

The Stormers decided to give it a try and went to meet Jac and his latest protégé. They got on very well and after a very short practice session The Stormers became Mike Berry's backing band. Bobby has very happy memories of Mike Berry but much less happy memories about another character who appeared on their musical vista.

A new generation of influences was beginning to emerge in the form of the independent record producer. The one that The Stormers met was a man named Joe Meek. Joe Meek made a considerable contribution to the music of the day and others have written of this else-where. The definitive biography by John Reptch tells an accurate, intriguing, and sometimes bizarre story of the catalogue of hits produced by Meek. Bobby, it has to be said, was never a fan of Mr Meek.

Joe Meek has variously been described as "a genius," "the British Phil Spector" and "a Svengali figure." Bobby Graham has used other descriptions, too. Joe Meek had been a staff engineer at Lansdowne Road Studios before setting up as an independent producer. Whilst at Lansdowne Road he had experimented with sound dis-tortion by allowing volume to increase beyond the upper limit of tolerance and into the saturation zone. This was not only against the house rules but, to the purist it was an act of musical heresy. It was to prove to be a very effective production tool.

Joe Meek had a studio in his flat at 304 Holloway Road, London. He had recently signed Mike Berry as a solo artist. Jac told Joe Meek that he had found a fantas-tic backing band so Joe asked them to attend his flat for an audition.

Bobby clearly remembers the day; not least because he remembers carrying his kit up a steep and narrow flight of stairs to the flat. The flat was on two floors with the studio on the upper floor. Joe had converted the 'spare' bedroom into a studio. All of the recording equipment was crammed into the small room with a spaghetti of cables trailing through the doorway into the adjoining room.

Bobby says that Joe was "a strange man" and, candidly, took an immediate dislike to him. His opinion never changed in the many dealings that ensued. In an endeavour to be objective Bobby does, though, acknowledge that Joe Meek was a considerable innovator and the products of his work form an impressive part of our pop music heritage.

Bobby later did a lot of recording at Joe Meek's flat, every time hauling his kit up the stairs. He did not always play the drums. Joe Meek was keen to produce new sounds; Bobby was often directed to play his drum cases. On another occasion Bobby remembers Joe Meek dashed into the room with a pair of pliers and asked Bobby to click them in time.

The audition went well. Joe Meek decided that he would like to sign the band but did not like their name. He decided that The Outlaws had a better ring to it and so Mike Berry and The Outlaws were formed. The first record they recorded together was a cover version of The Shirelles' 'Will You Love Me Tomorrow.' Prior to recording, the newly fledged Outlaws were given a single copy of the original and sent away to rehearse it. By the time of the recording session they were note perfect, but in the wrong key for Mike Berry. Reg Hawkins was uncharacteristically assertive and declined to delay recording while the band re-learned the number in a lower key. It is the recollection of some that Mike Berry struggled to record it at higher pitch than suited his voice. Mike Berry does not remember this late impediment being placed in his path and the record still sounds very good.

The arranger was a highly talented man named Charles Blackwell who worked with Joe Meek on many of his recordings. Bobby is a great admirer of Charles Blackwell of whom more later. Extraordinary though it may seem, the recording also used a string section who were crammed into another room at the studio. This added greatly to the sound. Mike Berry remembers the first recording and particularly The Outlaws.

"I met Bobby Graham first. I went to his house with Jac. Bobby had a piano there and he played the intro to 'What'd I Say'. I was pretty impressed. When we did the first recording session I was even more impressed; when I met them I think they were still called The Stormers. They were in a completely different league to any group I had worked with before. My own group was pretty Mickey Mouse but these guys were really good. Bobby Graham was a brilliant drummer. I remember being stuck in the corner miked up by Joe Meek for the first recording. Of course, I didn't know any different then and thought this was all perfectly normal. I was actually very pleased with the recording. I can also remember standing on the stairs when Joe Meek said "I think we should change our name like Holly/Berry and the group should be The Outlaws. No debate. It just happened."

Joe Meek was able to place the record with Decca who leased the track and issued it. Bobby Graham, and no doubt the others, listened avidly to Radio Luxemburg; he was delighted when the record received some airplay. Although the Mike Berry and The Outlaws version did not make the charts it made a sufficient impact for Joe Meek to decide to record further tracks. More than that, although no official pronouncement was made of the fact, The Outlaws became Joe Meek's house band.

Bobby should have been very happy, and was. But he was always uncomfortable with Joe Meek. Something that happened years later may serve to show that Bobby's discomfort, whilst instinctive, was not without a substantial evidential matrix. One of the tracks that The Outlaws later recorded, as a B side, was an instrumental called 'Crazy Drums' and was composed by Bobby Graham. The other members of the group liked the track and were unanimously of the view that this would be an ideal track to release as a B side. Joe Meek seemed happy with the decision; he approached Bobby saying that in order to sanction the decision he would have to be awarded half of the royalties. Bobby confesses to having been very naïve in those days; the prospect of seeing his name on the record seemed more important than the fact that he would be sharing the credit with 'Robert Duke', Joe Meek's nom de plume. Bobby blithely signed a contract in blank and was happy to see the names Duke and Graham on the record label. Years later when he had a fuller understanding of the music industry he rang the publishers, Ivy Music, and enquired why he had never received any royalties. They located the original contract. It contained only one name, Joe Meek.

After 'Will You Love Me Tomorrow' the next track they recorded with Mike Berry was called 'Swinging Low' which was a take on the anthem 'Swing Low Sweet Chariot'. This was long before it was adopted as the anthem of the England Rugby team and its supporters. Bobby remembers the publicity that Joe Meek organised for the record's launch. This involved a horse-drawn stagecoach being hauled down Oxford Street with The Outlaws dressed as cowboys and the track blasting from the stagecoach. The stunt attracted a lot of publicity but sadly the record did not make the charts.

However, chart success for Mike Berry and The Outlaws was just around the corner. The next three records were hits. The first, 'Tribute to Buddy Holly', entered the charts in October 1961, made Number 24 on the 12th of that month and stayed in the charts for six weeks. The song was written by Geoff Goddard; Mike Berry was the ideal choice to record the song because his voice sounded very like Buddy Holly. It also explains why Joe Meek had chosen Berry as Mike's new name. The Buddy Holly phenomenon had maintained its momentum since his death in a plane crash in February 1959. Although the record did not attract much critical acclaim, Bobby was ecstatic at having achieved chart success.

The next hit was not achieved until January of 1963, by which time Bobby had left The Outlaws. 'Don't You Think It's Time' entered the charts and went to Number 6 staying in the charts for twelve weeks. The interlude between the two was a long one; in the early 1960s a hit was always followed by a swift release of a follow up, preferably sounding as much like the original hit as possible. This was not so easy with a 'story' record. However, the second hit was soon followed by another. In April 1963 'My Little Baby' became a minor hit, charting at Number 34 and declining down the charts for seven weeks. That was the end of Mike Berry and The Outlaws' chart involvement although Mike Berry enjoyed modest success two decades later as a solo artist.

The chart success had a profound effect on the group's diary commitments; they found that gigs were plentiful and some of the venues were out of the top drawer. They regularly played the Assembly Rooms, Walthamstow, which was a major venue at the time and performed on the Granada Cinema circuit. The audiences were enthusiastic and the band had an impressive repertoire. Mike Berry was keen that they should perform at their best and he demanded that the band should assemble for sound checks well ahead of the gig.

Bobby always found this irksome as did the other Outlaws. In retrospect they all agree that Mike Berry was ahead of his time, a consummate professional striving for perfection. Bobby has only good things to say about Mike Berry and they remain firm friends.

Bobby Graham also found the travelling very hard. At the end of a gig he would be physically drained. Then, after packing his kit he had to drive either to the next venue or, more often, home, giving a lift to one or more members of The Outlaws. Billy Kuy remembers the end of one journey home: "It was about three o'clock in the morning and we had been travelling for hours; we were cold and tired and about a mile from where I was living

Bobby had to stop for some railway barriers that had closed for a train to pass. He said to me "you'll have to get out and walk. " I had my guitar and amp with me so I refused. Bobby drove on and we both got out of the car to unload my kit. I was so angry I punched him and gave him a really nasty black eye."

It is difficult to dovetail this into The Outlaws history; Billy Kuy recalls that this act of violence led to his being sacked from The Outlaws – "Joe Meek said he didn't like violence and that I would have to go." This is supremely ironic bearing in mind the circumstances surrounding Joe Meek's death less than decade later. However, Bobby Graham left The Outlaws some time before Billy Kuy so it seems that Billy Kuy's dismissal may have been a lingering one.

Bobby always enjoyed working with Charles Blackwell whom he describes as being very talented and a real gentleman. He was able to combine an easy going manner with the ability to inspire his players to play at their best. It helped that Charles Blackwell is an accomplished musician in his own right. Bobby worked with him a great deal throughout the 1960s. They keep in touch with each other; as Bobby candidly confesses, his behaviour later in the sixties cost him many friends so he is especially glad to remain friends with someone who was so influential upon his career.

It was Charles Blackwell who introduced the band to another artist who made a considerable impact on the charts in 1961. John Leyton was a young actor with a good singing voice who was chosen to record a song called 'Johnny Remember Me'. The song went to Number 1 and is remembered by many for the haunting female refrain of the song's title and John Leyton's strong melody. John Leyton has good reason to remember the recording even though, after forty years, detail is a bit fuzzy: "Really I was an actor who did some singing rather than a singer who did some acting. I thought The

Outlaws were great. The recording went well enough, Charles Blackwell was very helpful. I sang the song completely unaware what the finished article would turn out like. When I heard it I was amazed. I remember Bobby Graham at that session and the next one. He was a great drummer."

At the completion of the recording Bobby was entirely confident that this would be a hit and it was, not only reaching Number 1 but staying in the charts for a total of fifteen weeks, overlapping with the follow up hit 'Wild Wind', also backed, anonymously, by The Outlaws. This record made Number 2 in the charts; remaining in the charts for ten weeks, long enough to see the less memorable follow up 'Son This Is She' struggle to Number 15. This was recorded without The Outlaws backing.

Three people have memories of a week at the Gaiety Theatre in Chester. It was a Robert Stigwood production, John Leyton was topping the bill and was being backed by The Outlaws. Bobby had, by now, joined The Bruvvers and was taking advantage of a gap in Joe Brown's diary to join up with his old group for the week.

"When we got to Chester there were posters everywhere advertising the show," remembers John Leyton. "Unfortunately, they had spelt my name Layton. It was a lovely theatre and we were packed out every night. When Bobby Graham came on stage he had a completely shaved head. These days you wouldn't give it a second look but back then it was very unusual. It gave me some good lines with the audiences. I also remember The Outlaws were on fire and Bobby's drumming was superb."

Charles Blackwell was musical director at the show. He, too remembers, Bobby: "One evening as Bobby walked on stage he looked a bit unsteady; he had obviously been down the pub. The next thing I knew there was this almighty crash as Bobby fell into the drums and was sprawled all over the stage. He got up as though nothing had happened, sat on his stool and played beautifully. He couldn't walk but he could still play. Amazing."

Bobby has bittersweet memories of the week. "I had shaved my head the previous week in Birmingham. We were playing there with Joe. I asked him how he managed to get his hair to stick up like it did. He told me that what you had to do was shave your head and rub potato peelings into the scalp. I was pretty naïve and I believed him so I tried it. It didn't work. The following week at the Gaiety I was playing with The Outlaws but hadn't told Joe about it. He was pretty strict about these things and he probably wouldn't have agreed to me playing. One evening as the curtains opened guess who was sitting in the front row: Joe and his wife. He wasn't very happy."

John Leyton's chart success continued. He enjoyed another six chart entries over the next two years but never recaptured the success of his first two hits. He did though make a considerable success of his acting career, perhaps most notably for his playing the part of Willie the Tunnel King in the *The Great Escape* and for his major role in *Von Ryan's Express*. Interestingly, the game Trivial Pursuit attributes the former role, erroneously, to Charles Bronson. John Leyton was mildly embarrassed and a little miffed when, whilst playing the game, he answered "me" to the question "Who played Willie the Tunnel King in *The Great Escape?*" and then was deemed to be wrong!

So by the end of 1961 The Outlaws had made the charts and were developing a real reputation as being a versatile, tight band with a great ability to learn. The rhythm section was crucial to their success and Bobby was enjoying his playing. Billy Kuy recalls one of the innovations of the time: "I think Bobby was one of the first, if not the first, to augment the sound of the bass drum by taking off the front skin and putting an overcoat inside the drum. It made a very distinctive sound. The recording of the drums would be done with only three microphones, one for the bass drum, one for the snare and an overreaching one for the cymbals, nothing for the tom-toms or the hi-hat. It is amazing the way the records turned out with a really distinctive drum beat."

During 1961 Bobby was approached by a drum manufacturer and invited to endorse their new product range. The company was Carlton who were trying to break into the burgeoning market created by the plethora of groups that were springing up on both sides of the Atlantic. Carlton was a wholly-owned subsidiary of a company called John E. Dallas and, although well regarded, were anxious to improve their image. They were not yet one of the major players.

The proposal that was made to Bobby was an attractive one which he embraced enthusiastically. Bobby was invited to draw up his own specification and the kit was custom built. He specified a 26-inch bass drum, which although only two inches bigger in diameter than a standard bass drum, meant that the surface area of the drum skin was almost twenty per cent higher. This had a considerable effect on the sound. As well as a snare drum, there were two small tom-toms (which was unusual in 1961) as well as a bass tom-tom. Bobby even had his own monogrammed drumsticks. Bobby played Zildjian cymbals which were, and remain, the choice of most professional drummers. The kit was marketed as 'The Bob Graham Giant Kit'. It was, says Bobby, an excellent kit, used by him for the great majority of recordings during the 1960s and heard on many hit records. The connoisseur will detect the special sound the bass drum made.

Bobby Graham had by now become an assiduous listener of Radio Luxemburg which was a rich source of musical ideas for him. One artist that impressed him was Joe Brown. Joe Brown and his band The Bruvvers had enjoyed modest chart success with a, frankly, easily forgettable record called 'Darktown Strutters Ball' which spent six weeks in the charts and reached Number 34 in March 1960. His next hit was 'Shine' which also spent six weeks in the charts climbing one place higher than the predecessor.

Chart success was not the only measure of popularity; Joe Brown was widely recognised as an especially accomplished acoustic guitarist and was a very popular guest on television programmes, especially *The Jack Good Show*. Joe Brown has always enjoyed the respect and admiration of professional colleagues not simply because of his cheeky grin, cockney accent (although he was born in Lincolnshire) nor even his virtuoso guitar skills; he has always been the consummate professional. He is equally renowned as a hard taskmaster.

By the time of his second chart hit Joe Brown was looking for a new drummer. Charles Blackwell heard of the vacancy and suggested he might wish to invite Bobby Graham for an audition.

This is another audition that Bobby remembers well. It took place at the home of The Bruvvers' bass player, Pete Oakman, in Leytonstone. Bobby, characteristically, had rehearsed and was in good form. Joe Brown joined the rehearsal and was impressed with Bobby's playing. Bobby was impressed with Joe's height; somehow the television had made him seem less tall than he is. It was a meeting of minds and Bobby was offered the job as The Bruvvers' drummer.

This created one immediate problem and at least two more that surfaced in the following months. Bobby had not told The Outlaws about the audition. His natural reticence meant that he had not felt confident about being offered the job and so he had assumed he would not get it; so, with such anticipation he had not spoken to his colleagues. When he told them they were not best pleased. Joe Meek was not happy and said so. Bobby's relationship with him had never been good; Bobby, for once, was firm and direct. He said "Sorry Joe but I can't work with the group anymore and I don't want to work in your studios anymore." His choice of words, though infelicitous, was not deliberate but it conveyed the twin messages: sorry to leave The Outlaws, not sorry to leave Holloway Road.

And so Bobby became a Bruvver.

Joe Brown and The Bruvvers

Many medical practitioners subscribe to the view that the most effective piece of diagnostic equipment is the fictional 'retrospectoscope.' Using such a device makes Bobby realise that his days with The Bruvvers were "simply awesome". It did not always seem so at the time.

He joined Joe Brown and The Bruvvers in the autumn of 1961. After a very short period of rehearsal he felt he was fully integrated into the group and relished the prospect of the gruelling schedule that lay ahead. This was his first experience of being a member of a 'name' outfit and he determined to enjoy it and give it his all.

Joe Brown was a shrewd, though conspicuously fair, businessman who was more 'hands on' in his management than Bobby had expected. His financial acumen rose closer to the surface when Joe signed a management agreement with two equally shrewd agents, George Cooper and Harry Dawson. The Bruvvers were distinctly Joe Brown's backing group and not part of a financial entity with Joe Brown; this was not a co-operative organisation. Joe was the star and The Bruvvers were a separate unit. It followed he did not split his fee, nor any royalties, with the group. Instead, each member was paid a wage. Bobby had no complaints; it was a very good wage, rather more than he would have earned in any civilian job.

Of course, and yet again, hindsight beckons; in a different situation with better advice we all realise that a more financially adept group might have been able to negotiate a share of the royalties. Had this been so it would probably have proved to have been a better option, especially in the longer term. However, it was not an option that ever occurred to the members of the group and Bobby Graham was enormously proud to be playing with a headline band. In fact, although Joe Brown enjoyed considerable chart success, the pop charts were not the real measure of his talent or his enduring appeal.

A measure of his musical longevity is that, at the time of writing, he and Marty Wilde have just completed a sell out national tour, backed by The Bruvvers and The Wildcats although with none of their original members.

It should, perhaps, be made clear the description of this financial arrangement is not done in any pejorative way. It was neither unique nor even unusual. It was commonly the case that the public associated an individual singer as 'the star' notwithstanding the contribution made by the 'backing group.' This public perception may have been engineered by the record companies and maintained and often enhanced by the impresarios who arranged live performances and tours.

Of course there were exceptions, even in the 1950s. But as the decade became the Swinging Sixties a sea change was abroad. 'Backing groups' such as The Shadows acquired an identity of their own and have enjoyed spectacular success, recently completing their sell out 'Farewell Tour.' Others such as The Tremeloes enjoyed greater success as an entity than Brian Poole ever did when they were 'simply' his backing group. The real change came with the groups who wrote their own material and were well managed; The Beatles and The Rolling Stones spring readily to mind.

None of this was known to Bobby Graham as he embarked upon an exciting chapter in his life. Nationwide tours, radio, television, recording – and Bobby was only just twenty-one years of age. Nonetheless, he remembers that travel became a real challenge from the moment he joined The Bruvvers. He had thought touring with The Outlaws was tough but he was in for a major shock. Travel was no longer limited to two or three days (or, more often, nights) on the road.

Instead, they seemed constantly to be on the move; frequently they were away from home for seven nights a week, often for weeks at a time. It was not only live gigs, although there were plenty of those, but television and radio broadcasts, which were mostly live and "pretty scary" for all that, there were photo shoots and, of course, recording sessions.

Looking at a band's modern touring schedule, it is generally easy to discern that some thought has gone into all of the travelling implications; the venues follow a logical travel route with little retracing on the journey. Things were very different in the early sixties in many ways. Bobby remembers a particular example which was not untypical: Edinburgh on Monday, Southampton on Tuesday, Glasgow on Wednesday, Birmingham on Thursday, Leeds on Friday and two gigs in London on Saturday.

Of course, they were not the only outfit pursuing such a punishing travel schedule. There was a great fraternity amongst the majority of the groups and they were prescient in developing their networking skills. It may have seemed that it was just for food that they regularly stopped at the same transport cafes, in these largely pre-motorway days, but meeting other groups had other advantages too. Notes were compared about venues and audience reaction and it was not uncommon for the undervalued talents of individual players to be made known, often with beneficial consequences for the individual and sometimes dire consequences for the ungrateful.

One such favourite meeting place was The Blue Boar which was very close to the recently opened M1 motorway. The Blue Boar was a mecca for touring groups. The occasional zealous autograph hunter could reap rich rewards. It was, observes Bobby with a twinkle in his eye, at The Blue Boar that the concept of 'the groupie' first impacted upon his life; the term groupie had yet to be used but this was a semantic difference to the otherwise identical concept that the word now connotes.

Bobby Graham made his debut with Joe Brown and The Bruvvers at the Queens Theatre in Blackpool in late 1961. The gig was part of a tour promoted by an impresario named Larry Parnes. Parnes was an outstandingly successful promoter about whom much has been written. The epithet 'Parnes, Shillings and Pence' may have had some pejorative connotations but to the music fan he was a genius in putting together great value tours. It is no exaggeration to say that most of those that hit the charts in the late 1950s and early 1960s played on a Parnes-promoted tour. The bill would not simply comprise a headline group or artiste with a single supporting act. Often there would be ten or more acts on the same bill. Consequently journeys of many hundreds of miles would be undertaken in order for each individual or group to play as few as four songs.

Parnes had a great talent for leaving a space on the bill for the act that had shot to prominence in the weeks before, or even during, a tour. He would then offer an irresistible opportunity to join a major tour regardless of such other commitments that the new star they might have thought they were obliged to honour. Following his Queens Theatre debut, Bobby was to perform on innumerable Larry Parnes tours.

Joe Brown and The Bruvvers were a very slick act. Joe Brown had a highly charismatic stage presence, combining humour, interesting repertoire and great musical skills. The audience was invariably highly appreciative.

Typically, such a tour would include people of the calibre of Billy Fury, Eden Kane and Vince Eager with lots of American stars as well. It was interesting for Bobby that only a year before he had been backing artists copying some of these singers, now here he was playing with the original artist. It should have been unalloyed pleasure for Bobby. But the demons were still at work in his mind and he fought hard to concentrate on his music and the golden opportunity that had been presented to him. In fact, Bobby enjoyed these tours because he did not have to drive as much as he had done in the past. For most of the time he played with The Outlaws and before them The Stormers, he was the only one who could drive.

For the many long journeys that were involved, Larry Parnes would insist that all of the musicians and singers travel by coach. He, of course, never travelled that way. Bobby could rarely sleep on these long coach journeys through the night but he did not see this as a problem. He has an abiding recollection of one such journey. Bobby found himself sitting on a double seat with Karl Denver, who, although mostly remembered for his falsetto rendition of 'Wimoweh', his greatest hit, did, in fact reach the top twenty with his first five record releases. Karl Denver was a Glaswegian who found no difficulty in sleeping on coaches. Across, the aisle was Eden Kane who was enjoying the fruits of his success, having reached Number 1 in June 1961 with his first hit 'Well I Ask You.' He reached the top ten with each of his five hits. Eden Kane spent much of his travelling time reading books.

Billy Fury was on the same coach, playing cards with his road manager. Billy Fury became a legend; his career having started, so it is said, after it was pointed out to him that he had more than a passing resemblance to Eddie Cochran. Until that time, the story goes, the young Ronald Wycherley had had no musical aspirations. However, by February 1959 he had hit the charts with 'Maybe Tomorrow': He was still only seventeen years of age. In the 1960s he scored more hits than any of his fellow Liverpudlians, including The Beatles. He never hit the Number 1 spot although he made Number 2 with 'Jealousy' in September 1961, having made Number 3 less than four months earlier with (probably) his most famous hit 'Halfway To Paradise.' He made Number 3 twice more and spent a total of two hundred and eighty one weeks in the charts. At the back of the coach Del

Shannon was stretched out across the back seat, fast asleep. Of course, Joe Brown was also there. He spent much of his travelling time quietly picking at his acoustic guitar, honing his already highly-developed skills.

By now Bobby was, or at least should have been, well adjusted to his changed identity. It was not unusual for musicians to play under a stage name. However, there were many times when his sense of introspection made him feel like little Bobby Neate from Edmonton and he wondered to himself whether he really belonged in the music business. Although an objective assessment of his playing would leave the listener with no doubt, Bobby had plenty of insecurities, though, at least temporarily allayed by his pleasure at being in the company of The Bruvvers.

The band at that time were Keith Charles on rhythm guitar, Pete Oakman on bass guitar and Bobby Graham on drums; Joe Brown was the vocalist and played lead guitar. He always played an amplified acoustic guitar rather than a solid-bodied model. Not long after Bobby joined, Keith Charles left the group and was replaced by Johnny Beverage.

For the Christmas/New Year Season of 1961-2 Joe Brown and The Bruvvers were booked for a seven week pantomime season at Stockton on Tees; they then moved to Hull for a further three weeks. The pantomime played for six days each week and there were gigs on almost every Sunday evening, playing all over the country.

The pantomime was *Aladdin* with Joe Brown playing the part of Wishy Washy. Bobby was given the part of 'A Chinese Policeman' which involved a single line. At the end of the pantomime proper Joe Brown and The Bruvvers played a set based upon their stage act but playing more numbers than on the tours.

Although there was some comfort to be derived from the fact that a 'season' reduced the travelling, there were still periods of intense boredom. Theatrical landladies were the butt of jokes; the truth was not so funny. The landlady at Stockton insisted that her 'guests' left by 9.30 am and were not allowed back until after the show had ended. The irony was that there was then often a restriction upon arriving back later than a certain time.

Bobby tried to alleviate the boredom by spending time in his dressing room making model cars. He was by now a regular heavy drinker who frequently steadied his nerves with alcohol before playing. One day he was introduced to Newcastle Brown Ale. He drank about eight bottles before realising how potent it was; by this time it was too late. He arrived late on stage, was incapable of managing his single line and was rescued only by the quick thinking Joe Brown who made the line his own.

This incident is etched on Bobby's memory. The following day he was confronted by an irate Joe Brown who made his views clear. He would not allow Bobby to compromise the group's professionalism. Joe himself remembers the incident well. He declines the opportunity to criticise Bobby unduly, remembering him instead as a brilliant drummer.

"Of course, I should have realised that he wasn't just thinking of himself; I am sure he had my best interests at heart too. I was just too stupid and pig headed to realise it." Bobby is grateful, too, to the other Bruvvers who rallied round and did their best to heal the potential rift that had been created by the discovery of Bobby's problem with alcohol.

During their down time the group were active in pursuit of their musical ambitions. For Bobby it was mostly practising; for others, in particular Pete Oakman and Johnny Beverage, it was song writing and composing. It was Pete Oakman and Johnny Beverage who wrote 'A Picture of You' which is still clear in the public's memory as the distillation of all of the group's success. The song was written at Peter Oakman's home, composed on his upright piano. Pete, who remains in regular contact with Bobby, still maintains that it only took about twenty minutes to write.

They played the song to Joe Brown who liked it. They recorded a 'demo' which they played to Ray Horrocks, the Artist and Repertoire Manager at Pye Records. He "absolutely loved it" and arranged a hurried session to record it. It was recorded at the Pye Studios at Bryanston Street in London. It was one of four tracks recorded at the same session. Another track which, was already a stage favourite, was 'All Things Bright and Beautiful'. Although recorded at the Pye Studios it was released on Pye's sister label Piccadilly. It was a smash hit and reached Number 2 in May 1962, staying in the charts for nineteen weeks.

This was the second of their four chart entries that year; 'What a Crazy World We're Living In' reached Number 37 in January, in September 'Your Tender Look' reached Number 31 and 'It Only Took a Minute' entered the charts in November, reaching Number 6 the following month.

It was 'A Picture of You' that elevated Joe Brown into the premier league of pop musicians. This increased the already demanding work schedule and added a new 'problem' for them. Merely getting in and out of theatres was no longer the cakewalk it had been hitherto. It was an especial problem for Joe because his face and hairstyle made him a particularly conspicuous individual; what many people didn't realise until they saw him close up was quite how tall he is. He found visiting restaurants to be very different after 'A Picture of You' made him so famous.

Bobby enjoyed playing all of the numbers; to many it is his tight drumming on their next hit 'That's What Love Will Do', which reached Number 3 in February 1963 that was marking him out as an outstanding studio as well as stage drummer.

The musical director on most of these sessions was the "amazingly talented" Les Reed. He achieved distinction with Tom Jones' first hit 'It's Not Unusual' which reached Number 1 in the charts in 1965 and launched Jones the

Voice onto the world. In fact years before this Les Reed was known to be a very talented and innovative musician. He had played piano with The John Barry Seven and moved into session work with conspicuous success.

Whilst they were recording 'A Picture of You' another Pye staff arranger and A&R man, Tony Hatch, had slipped into the control box. He asked Bob Auger, who was the recording engineer on the session who the drummer was. "That's Bobby Graham" replied Auger. Hatch asked for Bobby Graham's phone number. He told Bob Auger that he thought Bobby had the potential for session work. Although he was right, he did not make contact for over a year. When he did make contact he was influential in introducing Bobby to the world of the studio musician or 'session man.'

'What a Crazy World' was actually recorded live at the Globe Theatre in Stockton. Although its chart success was modest, it was (and remains) a great favourite played to live audiences. The reference to "Me Bruvvers are all layabouts" was always accompanied by Joe giving a nod and a wink to the audience who reacted with great enthusiasm. Joe Brown and The Bruvvers played the most eclectic mix of music. Their set regularly included the instrumental 'Hava Nagila', an old Hebrew folk tune, which showed what an accomplished guitarist Joe Brown is. His guitar skills were also prominent on 'An English Country Garden' which, played acoustically, was also a great shop window for his talent. To dive straight into a Chuck Berry classic such as 'Sweet Little Sixteen' showed a diversity which was, frankly, not always obvious in all hit groups of the day.

Following 'That's What Love Will Do', Joe Brown and The Bruvvers were less successful with their next two releases 'Nature's Time for Love' and 'Sally Ann' making 26 and 28 in the charts. Although Joe Brown had two more hits as a solo artist in 1967 and 1973, Joe Brown and The Bruvvers' chart success was over by the autumn of 1963.

During 1963 Bobby's drinking began to become a major problem. He was a natural introvert but drink changed his personality. Superficially, he became an extrovert, but it wasn't as simple as that. Allied to the extrovert personality was the darker side. Bobby became aggressive and belligerent and, occasionally, violent. He was drinking every day and, worse, was becoming a secret and devious drinker, concealing bottles in his drum cases and seeking to avoid others knowing how much he was drinking.

Like most 'secret' drinkers, the secret got out. Joe realised that Bobby was drinking and that this risked compromising the musical integrity of The Bruvvers. There were a number of disagreements and then a showdown. Joe Brown was firm, fair but resolute: Bobby had to go: "It was a great shame. Bobby was a brilliant drummer and most of the time I really liked him and we got on well. The trouble was I never knew what he was up to. In the end I had to decide what my priorities were – it was Bye Bye Bobby."

Bobby had loved his time with the group, he had made many friends and learned a great deal about the music industry. His playing had been acknowledged and admired by many famous artists and, although he didn't know it, fresh challenges were just around the corner.

So, coincidentally with the ending of their run of hits, Bobby Graham's time as a Bruvver came to an end. Drink had created another musical casualty.

Life After The Bruvvers

Curiously, losing his job with The Bruvvers seemed not to worry Bobby at all. In the tightly-knit musical world in which he moved he already had an excellent name as a drummer and he had, thus far, been able to conceal the extent of his drinking from most of the people that mattered. He acknowledges that he was regarded as "a bit of a handful" but this did not detract from his appeal to prospective employers. Really good drummers were not that easy to find so Bobby was in heavy demand.

"In a sense it was too easy. If I had had to struggle to get work I might have appreciated it more when I got it. As it was, I adopted a sort of easy-come, easy-go attitude."

Offers of work came in as soon as it was known that Bobby was available. Flatteringly, a number of the offers came from artists with whom he had toured when he had played with Joe Brown and The Bruvvers. "Peer recognition in the music business is very important and so to be offered work by someone who has heard you play six or seven nights a week for thirteen weeks is very nice."

Amongst those who asked Bobby to play with them were Karl Denver and Eden Kane. Bobby was tempted by both of these offers; he liked and respected them both and felt he would enjoy playing with either. However, after only very brief deliberation he chose another offer; he joined Marty Wilde and became part of his backing group The Wildcats.

Marty Wilde was a very interesting man and someone of whom Bobby became a great admirer as well as a firm friend. He was another of those discovered and promoted by Larry Parnes and one of the first to undergo an enforced name change. So, Reg Smith became Marty

Wilde. In fact, the young singer had already recognised that his birth name did not have much of a cachet to it so was performing as Reg Patterson when Parnes discovered him singing at a club in Soho.

Marty Wilde made his name with the youth of the UK by his regular appearances on Jack Good's *Six Five Special*. His third single was a very effective cover of Jody Reynolds' American hit 'Endless Sleep'. Many believe it be an improvement on the original; it was his first hit, reaching Number 4 in the charts in the summer of 1958 and remaining in the charts for fourteen weeks. After two numbers that did not reach the charts in March the following year he was back in the top five with 'Donna.' This was followed by with three more top ten hits 'A Teenager in Love,' 'Sea of Love' and 'Bad Boy,' all of them in 1959.

Chart success continued, although not at quite such a high level. January 1961 saw him reach Number 9 with a cover version of the Bobby Vee hit 'Rubber Ball.' Extraordinarily, by modern standards there were two versions of the same song in the top ten at the same time. Bobby Vee, a photogenic American teenager (who had once included a young Robert Zimmerman in his backing group) reached Number 4 in the UK charts. Marty Wilde never reached the top thirty after that, not even with his 1968 release, 'Abergavenny.' He has an enduring appeal as a stage and concert performer.

Marty Wilde had followed Jack Good from BBC to ITV when, with a remarkable inability to understand or anticipate the power of the teenage market, BBC had decided that they could do without Jack Good. His *Oh Boy* show was a massive hit on the commercial channel and became a showcase for the UK's burgeoning pop music talent.

Marty was not just a performer, he was, and remains, an accomplished writer too, latterly writing many of the hits for his polymath daughter Kim. It was Marty's writing that provided Bobby's introduction to The

Wildcats. The original line-up of The Wildcats had included Big Jim Sullivan on lead guitar, Brian Bennett on drums and Licorice Locking on bass guitar. Big Jim Sullivan, whilst best known as a session guitarist (many say the session guitarist), also had an illustrious career after he left Marty Wilde. Brian Bennett and Licorice Locking replaced Tony Meehan and Jet Harris after they left the Shadows to become a highly successful duo.

The new Wildcats line-up that Bobby joined was Phil Dennis on piano, Rex Oates on bass guitar and Tony Oakman (brother of Pete who had written 'A Picture of You' for Joe Brown), on bass. Bobby has happy memories: "It was great. There were no egos in the group, we were just a bunch of guys having a great time and enjoying our music too."

Marty Wilde wrote an instrumental number called 'Polaris' (about which more later) which was recorded by The Wildcats under the name 'The Boys.' There was great excitement in the group when they discovered that the producer was to be John Barry who was already widely acknowledged within the music industry as a major player. The recording was made at the EMI Studios; it was not a hit although well-received by the music critics.

Bobby found his days on the road with Marty to be great fun. They continued on the Larry Parnes Rock and Roll Circus all over the UK for six months. The format of the tours was almost identical to his time with The Bruvvers but somehow Bobby found it more relaxed.

"Marty was not so demanding as Joe had been; he used to laugh very easily and quite often we travelled in his car rather than on the tour coach. I really enjoyed it."

Curiously, in the light of how Bobby's career was to develop, The Wildcats did not record with Marty Wilde; he used session musicians.

Bobby looks back at his private life at the time without much pride. He had married secretary June Day in

August of 1962, with Joe Brown as his best man. The next year he had become a father to Tracy; but neither of these events had caused him to change his ways at all. He, his wife and baby daughter were living in a tiny rented flat in Chingford. He was earning very good money but June saw little enough of it. Bobby was drinking heavily, on tour he lived the life of a single man and when not on tour he was spending late evenings and early mornings in clubs. Much of the day, if not working, he spent in pubs.

He felt the need to have the trappings of success: "It was more important to have a flash car parked outside the flat than it was to have a decent flat." He also suffered the common drinker's condition of impulse buying: "Sometimes I would see some gadget that was new to the market and I would think 'I've got to have that, how have I managed without one' but by the time I got home I would think 'what the hell did I buy that for.'"

After six months with The Wildcats Bobby had had enough of the continual and gruelling schedule of touring and so he left, on very good terms. Marty Wilde was very understanding and he and Bobby remain good friends.

The John Barry Seven

It was not only Tony Hatch that spotted Bobby Graham's potential when Bobby was playing with Joe Brown and The Bruvvers. Ray Horrocks, a staff producer at Pye Records, asked Bobby if he would like to play on an instrumental album to be recorded by Davy Graham. Bobby readily agreed and retains an abiding recollection of arriving at the studio anticipating being a small part of a considerable ensemble. Instead it was just Bobby and Davy Graham.

Davy Graham (who was no relation to Bobby) was an acoustic guitarist with a fantastic talent and a very wide repertoire. He and Bobby hit it off immediately and the product of the session was an excellent album called *The Guitar Player*. This was released towards the end of 1962 and, whilst not a huge commercial success, it has become a collectors' item. This was Bobby's first 'real' session work.

As an aside, Davy Graham had a effect on another aspiring guitarist. One night, probably in 1963, at the Richmond Jazz Club, the members of Dave Hunt's Blues Band were pausing between sets. Someone asked their rhythm guitarist if his friend could borrow his guitar. The imitation Gretsch was played by Davy Graham like never before; the audience was stunned at his virtuosity. Its owner was also stunned; his name was Ray Davies.

John Barry had spotted Bobby Graham at the recording of 'Polaris' the instrumental written by Marty Wilde. It was, fairly transparently, a response to the outstandingly successful Joe Meek/Tornadoes success 'Telstar', which had reached Number 1 in 1962 and spent twenty-five consecutive weeks in the charts. Bobby is firmly of the view that John Barry had inspired Marty Wilde to write 'Polaris' deliberately to annoy Joe Meek, who had a deep suspicion of John Barry. It bordered on paranoia; he frequently complained that Barry was stealing all his ideas. In fact, John Barry had an original talent and vision of his own.

Bobby Graham preferred the B side of 'Polaris' to the main track itself. The B side had an almost Jet Harris six string bass sound; this track attracted virtually no air play; B sides rarely did.

John Barry was another musical genius. He was born John Barry Prendergast in November 1933. He came from an entertainment family in that his father owned a number of cinemas in the North of England. John Barry was an enthusiastic music student whilst at school and then was fortunate to study full time at York Minster. He became an accomplished pianist, schooled in classical music and developed into a multi-instrumentalist when his introduction to jazz encouraged him to learn to play the trumpet. This added to the number of instruments on which he was already a virtuoso.

In the early 1950s John Prendergast was called up for his National Service and took advantage of the musical opportunity this presented by forming a jazz band. By the time he was demobbed the musical complexion in the United Kingdom had changed radically. John Prendergast espoused the new sounds and within a very short time he had assembled his first 'Seven.' He adopted the shorter form of his name and they became The John Barry Seven. His band was soon spotted by Jack Good, who was then producing the famous *Six Five Special* and who was looking for musicians for the programme. The John Barry Seven were not initially chosen for the pro-gramme, perhaps because of the similarity of their sound with that of the then resident band Don Lang and his Frantic Five.

A few months later, with a slightly altered musical bias, The John Barry Seven were offered and accepted the musical residency on the show. Thereafter, they supported dozens of aspiring pop stars, many of whom achieved stellar success; others less so.

John Barry has had a distinguished career but remains best known for his work on the guitar driven James Bond Theme, which was written by Monty Norman and played by the brilliant guitarist Vic Flick. John Barry also entered almost every home in the land in the early sixties having composed and played 'Hit And Miss' which was itself a top ten hit and which became the theme tune for the David Jacobs presented *Juke Box Jury*.

During the recording of 'Polaris', Bobby and John Barry found that they worked well together; their mutual respect and musical empathy developed into a firm friendship. Bobby soon learned that John was also a huge fan of The Stan Kenton Orchestra, an American band that had been together for many years and who had been successful in every sphere of big band music. When Bobby discovered that John Barry had studied musical arranging under the tutelage of a member of The Stan Kenton Orchestra he was enraptured.

Bobby recalls a number of occasions when he visited John Barry at his London flat and the two would sit listening to Stan Kenton records and talk music for hours.

"John was a very quiet fellow but his depth of musical knowledge and the breadth of his musical ideas were simply phenomenal. Many clever musicians see in only one direction; John seemed to see in every direction."

Bobby remembers that it was at John Barry's flat one evening that he was paid one of the greatest and most meaningful compliments of his career. To the best of his recollection Bobby remembers John Barry saying "You know, you have an immense talent for such a young person. You are one of the greatest drummers I have heard in my career in the music industry." Bobby was struck dumb but the compliment was stored in the deeper reaches of his memory and it came back to his conscious recollection years later when he was going through troubled times.

One evening, probably in 1963, when dining in a restaurant together, John Barry told Bobby that he was going to Ember Records as an arranger and producer. He said that he would very much like it if Bobby joined him, both to play on the recordings and also to do some production work. It seemed a wonderful opportunity.

It was while working at Ember Records that John Barry approached Bobby with another proposal. The John Barry Seven was still immensely popular as a live band, especially on the university and college circuit but John Barry's many other commitments made it very difficult for him personally to tour with the band. He proposed a solution. He asked Bobby Graham to take over the running of The John Barry Seven and to act as the band's musical arranger and director. Bobby jumped at the chance and so took over the band's heavy diary schedule, too. There was one problem. For very good reasons it was important that the band's identity as The John Barry Seven should remain. Contractually, those that had booked The John Barry Seven expected The John Barry Seven to be the band that appeared at the gig. Secondly, they had a very good name and it was wise to retain the reputation and fund of goodwill that went with it. There was absolutely nothing wrong with what they did because their musical direction, ethos and existence were under the ultimate control and direction of John Barry; they were still his Seven.

It was decided to recruit a new trumpet player to take over the personal role of John Barry. Bobby Graham and others, supported by common sense, dictated that it would be prudent to find a replacement that physically resembled the band's founder. It was decided to hold auditions. One of the players who attended the audition was a young man named Alan Bown. Bobby felt that he had exactly what was needed.

"He looked a bit like John Barry, he was tall, on the skinny side and, just like John, he didn't thrust himself to front of stage. He sort of blended into the background, just like John Barry himself, because for all his undoubted musical prowess, John was always happy to be one of the band and not the band."

So Alan Bown got the job. In fact, he was not the only new recruit. Since it had become clear that John Barry did not have time to tour, the band had nominally lain dormant and 'rested' but in reality had disbanded, with the other band members moving on in different directions. Another new recruit was Ray Russell whom Bobby remembers was a very fine guitarist and who later went on to become a very accomplished composer and arranger. Initially, Bobby hesitated because he wasn't convinced that Ray Russell's image was quite right: "How can I put it kindly? He was a bit on the large side." But Bobby was so impressed with his enthusiasm and the quality of his playing that he took a chance, something he never regretted. "He was a fine player, utterly reliable and dependable and he also had a wicked sense of humour."

With the completion of the line-up of the 'John Barry Seven' Bobby found himself back on the road. The venues were different to the mainstream venues that he had been used to playing, but he found the student audiences highly appreciative of the music that was played.

"Many is the time that Alan Bown was asked for his autograph; he never disappointed the fans, always dutifully signing 'John Barry.' I am not sure what the real John would have said if he found out. We would be at a university hundreds of miles out of London and John Barry would be back at his flat in Sloane Square."

Playing, arranging and directing The John Barry Seven kept Bobby pretty active, but he still occasionally found time to play with other groups on an ad hoc basis. This was a very busy period in Bobby's life.

On top of everything else Bobby also found time to do

some jamming, impromptu playing, at a very popular venue called Annie's Room. 'Annie' was Annie Ross who recorded at Ember Records. She was part of the "amazing" jazz vocal trio Lamberts, Hendricks and Ross. She was a highly-regarded singer and a very popular lady so it surprised no-one that Annie's Room was an instant success with the musical fraternity and show business folk generally. People partied all night.

"I went there many times and sat in with some wonderful artists. The resident organist was guy called Alan Haven who I later produced for Fontana Records. I often used to play with him but also with myriad others who would just pop in and play."

The most memorable of these spontaneous sessions occurred when Bobby was jamming to a capacity audience. "In walked Sammy Davies Junior. I was a big fan so was delighted to see him. If memory serves, he was with Jimmy Tarbuck and I am sure Kenny Lynch was there too. Sammy obviously liked the sound we were making because in no time he was up on stage singing to an enthralled audience. What a buzz I got out of that."

His duties at Ember Records also brought some other interesting personalities into his purview. One of the most colourful was Mandy Rice Davies. She had risen to public prominence as the result of the Profumo Affair which had gripped the nation in 1963. She and the even more famous (or notorious) Christine Keeler had had a mixed press as the result of their involvement. Mandy Rice Davies, whom the press described as "an unemployed eighteen-year-old actress" gave evidence for the prosecution at the Old Bailey Trial of 'Dr' Stephen Ward. In answer to a question which contained a proposition contrary to the evidence she had given, she used an expression which has passed into everyday usage: "Well he would say that wouldn't he?"

Her minor stardom led her to make a record. Bobby was asked to produce. "She was a real joy to work with she really was. She was really bubbly and had a great personality. She was also very determined with what she wanted to do with her life and, for my part that meant making a good record."

Bobby produced an Extended Play record; of the four tracks 'You've Got What It Takes' and 'Love For Sale' are memorable, the other tracks less so. The recording session took place at the old Olympic Studios in London. The musical director was Arthur Greenslade and the engineer Keith Grant. Bobby had no difficulty in assembling a team of session players.

"When the session players found out that the recording artist was Mandy Rice Davies they all wanted to be in on it." In spite of the nation's prurient interest, the record was not a bestseller in the UK although, curiously, it was awarded a gold disc for sales in Italy.

After about a year, Bobby and John Barry made an amicable decision to part company. Bobby remembers their time together with great affection and remains a great admirer of John Barry who "is still writing great music for great movies."

A Recording Session

Much of what is written presupposes that everyone can visualise a recording session. True, almost everyone with any musical interest must have seen television or film clips of recording sessions. We see singers wearing headphones singing into strange looking microphones while sundry others casually drape themselves over randomly placed chairs or studio equipment. Nonetheless, it has been Bobby Graham's experience that many ask the question "what was a recording session really like in the sixties?"

Musical purists may baulk at the superficiality and broad generalisations that this chapter includes. Its purpose is not to provide a definitive exposition of how all sessions were recorded, rather to provide an insight into how it was normally done. Bobby played on thousands of sessions and agrees that no two were identical.

"The first thing you have got to remember is that everything that was recorded was played by live musicians. In those days there were no samples, no synthesisers – everything was played live. So if the producer wanted to have the sound of a seventy piece orchestra, then that is what he booked. If he needed a string section with twelve musicians then twelve string players would be brought in."

The session would be overseen by the A&R man who was also called the producer. A&R was 'Artist and Repertoire' and he would set the whole thing up. He was, in Bobby's words, the complete boss. The most famous A&R man of the era was almost certainly Sir George Martin. The A&R man would liaise with the individual artist, ensure that he was signed up for the particular session and make sure that he was properly coached in anticipation of the session. He would also have the responsibility for ensuring the suitability of the material to be recorded. In the early sixties it was not usual for the artists to have written their own material although this was subject to phenomenal and rapid change over the next couple of years. Some A&R men wrote their own material, sometimes there were in-house writers and much material came from outside publishers. A rich source of material was America. It was extremely common to do cover versions of American hits.

Assembling the session musicians would be the next step. The procedure would vary depending on the nature of the session. If it were simply a rhythm section (comprising bass guitar, guitars and piano) then the A&R man might organise it by making direct contact with the players. If it were a large session, especially one with orchestral support, then the A&R man would use a 'fixer' to book and coordinate the attendance of the musicians.

Usually, although not always, there would be a musical director. The ones about which most is written in this book are Les Reed, Arthur Greenslade and Charles Blackwell. They would be in contact with the A&R man and discuss what was needed for the session; they would set out their musical requirements, often advocating an individual musician for a particular session or even for a specific track. The musical director would also be in contact with the producer of the tracks to be recorded and always the engineer who would be responsible for handling the recording equipment. At the session there was often considerable blurring of the edges of the roles of the musical director and producer; what mattered was that they should work in harmony to achieve the desired sound. Although their positions in the musical hierarchy were acknowledged by all present, the lines of demarcation of responsibility were not strictly adhered to.

On the day of the recording the A&R man would be in the recording box, which is the production room, and then would almost invariably start by getting a balance and sound from the rhythm section although this might not be the case if there was an orchestra to be recorded.

The producer would gradually work the sound of the band or orchestra through a mixing desk which would allow for later manipulation. The producer would normally stay in the control room. However, musical directors liked to be in the studio itself. Some musical directors played a literally hands-on role; Arthur Greenslade often played piano on tracks for which he was the musical director. The musicians would be able to hear what each other was doing through headphones ('cans'). Everything would be recorded through the mixing desk on to separate tracks on the multi track recorder.

The classical orchestra players were very often reluctant pop musicians; they were all able to sight read music, respond to musical direction and, in theory, play their parts impeccably each time. The backing track(s) would, though, precede the addition of the vocals so that the singer was singing to the full backing sound.

As the result of a binding agreement with the Musicians Union, every artist was obliged to sing 'live' during the recording with musicians. It was, though, common knowledge to the session men that as soon as they left the studio the artist would re-record their voice until the producer had the best performance that he could get from them.

So all of the musical backing was now recorded on separate tracks into the mixing desk. The manipulation process would not be embarked upon at that stage but would be dealt with after the musicians had left. Even in the sixties this could be very sophisticated. Not only did it allow the engineer to raise or lower the volume of any track, perhaps to add to the power of a drum beat, or bring a guitar solo to greater prominence, it could also create a stereo and echo effects either throughout the whole of the track or for a chosen musical sequence.

After the musicians had been recorded, the vocals

would be dubbed on to the backing tracks. The ordinary perception of this process is that the vocalist would go into a vocal booth and lay down the track from start to finish. Very often this was not how it was done. Sometimes the recording was done in very short sequences until each sequence was deemed right. Then it would be up to the producer to choose the sequences that he wanted to aggregate to make the whole.

"A lot of these singers had very little or no studio experience. I used to get very nervous for myself, for some of those studio virgins the experience must have been terrifying. There is a great difference between singing to an adoring audience, especially one with screaming girls, and being in a studio under the scrutiny of these dedicated professionals."

After the vocals had been dubbed there would be a mixing session. The whole recording was put through the mixing desk again. The A&R man and the engineer re-equalized the sound until they had the sound they liked.

Sometimes, they would not be satisfied with what they had; they would have travelled in a full circle and decided that they wanted to re-record the drums, for example. This was not because of any deficiency in the player's playing but because the almost-finished product may not have turned out as originally envisaged

Charles Blackwell remembers some late night sessions with Bobby Graham: "Apart from anything else it was physically demanding. Often by the time of these over-dubs, adding the drums to the almost complete track, Bobby would have been on the go all day, playing at three different studios during the day and then meeting me at 10 o'clock at night to set up his kit and play for another few hours. Some very successful tracks were finished in this way. Often it would just be me, Bobby and the engineer. Somehow it was nice to be adding the final polish to something that you were then happy with."

After everyone was happy this 'final version' would

then be sent to be made into a master acetate from which the individual discs were pressed.

Bobby Graham has recorded in five decades and has seen some "unbelievable changes ... the contrast from what there was then to what there is now is probably best shown by the influence that computers and digital recording techniques have made. Now you can have the sound of a seventy piece orchestra in your computer. I don't think it's as much fun."

The Fixer

The Fixer played an important role in 1960s session music. The Fixer was the generic name for the person who liaised with the musical arranger/director and the individual session musician; he coordinated the requirements of the former with the abilities of the latter. His was a pivotal role and was of great value to producer and player alike. Although the fundamental nature of 'The Fixer's' work was transparent, he deliberately ensured that the precise working methods and access to his contact book were opaque.

In 1960s London there was no more influential fixer than Charlie Katz, of whom many would say he was 'the' fixer. Charlie was an extraordinary man, Machiavellian in many ways, but with the great facility of meeting the needs of the musical arranger and, mostly, keeping the player reasonably happy, too. He was by profession a violinist who had his own orchestra, The Charlie Katz Orchestra, and he had a regular early morning slot on the radio. This was in the days when there was only the BBC with their limited programming and was still some years short of the launch of Radio One, Two, Three and Four in September 1967. Charlie Katz's network of contacts was simply awesome; this explains in large measure why he achieved such dominance in a tightly knit musical community. He worked on a freelance basis and was proud to boast that his services were available to all. In many respects he had control of the destiny of a great many session and other players. It was in his gift as to whether any musician would play at any session.

Elsewhere in this book a 'typical' day in Bobby's professional life is described. Frequently, he would play on three sessions, one morning, one afternoon and one evening; often at three studios some miles apart. In order to understand the complexity of the fixer's role it is necessary to extrapolate a Bobby Graham day. This can be done by factoring in the services of any other musicians who would be required at one, two or three of those same sessions; additionally, some of those players may be required to play at others sessions being recorded at other studios the same day. Perhaps in these computer driven days the complexity of the fixer's role seems less than it was; in the pen, pad and notebook days of the sixties, it was a formidably challenging exercise.

The individual demands of the arranger would not be confined to requests for, say, "a rhythm section for Studio Three at Decca." Typical request might specify "lead guitar, rhythm guitar (although not always called such) bass guitar, piano, drums and a seventy piece orchestra." Charlie would arrange it; it was a very rare event that Charlie did not muster the required players.

There were two obvious consequences for the player; if Charlie liked you and you played well then work was plentiful. The corollary of this proposition is obvious; if Charlie didn't like you or you didn't play well then Charlie might decline to book you. Indeed, Bobby's perception is that Charlie employed a punishment regime which was not necessarily directly related to a player's session skills.

"If you weren't up to it musically then he wouldn't use you: full stop. But even if you were playing well and you did something to upset him then he would put you 'on holiday' for a couple of weeks; I think he did this just to show who was controlling the purse strings. With a lot of players it worked and they were really deferential to Charlie. With me it had the opposite effect; I didn't like him anyway and if he tried it on with me I let him know my views."

Of course, the fixer was not omnipotent. Nor did he

always have the first or last say in who should play on any session. It was frequently the case that a musical director would make specific requests for individual players for particular sessions. A familiar, and formidable line-up was often specified: Vic Flick, Big Jim Sullivan, Jimmy Page, Alan Weighell, Eric Ford, Arthur Greenslade and Bobby Graham.

In a sense this eased Charlie Katz's duties; he had a nice tight unit that had the skills and versatility to play almost everything and so it was frequently the case that, at least the core of this unit would follow each other around London on a three session day. It also meant that so far as Bobby Graham and some of the other great players were concerned, their abilities were such that they were in demand by the major producers of the day. Hence Bobby's sometimes disrespectful attitude to Charlie Katz did not restrict the demand for his playing.

One of the deliberately obscure aspects of the fixer's role was the financial one and, to this day, Bobby is unclear as to how the financial arrangements worked.

"Obviously the fixer had to take his cut but we were never sure if we were paid a specific sum from which he took his cut or whether he agreed a sum with the arranger and paid us a proportion of it. We didn't really care. It wasn't a money thing for any of us; we were happy to be doing what we were doing and anyway the money that we were paid was good."

Payment was made at the end of each session with Charlie rushing round the studio distributing sealed brown envelopes to the individual musicians like a whirling wages clerk. That the payments were made in this way has by caprice and serendipity, served to rob us of a rich part of our musical heritage. The fact that at the end of the session each player was paid and nothing was owed to anyone meant that it was wholly unnecessary for the studio, the musician or even Charlie Katz to keep records of which musician played on which recording.

Presumably Charlie kept some records but for his own accounting purposes rather than for posterity. Had a different payment method been employed then there exists at least the possibility that a documentary record would survive of who played on what.

Bobby is not alone in having an incomplete recall of the sessions he played at or the tracks he played on. This is commonly the case with the session players. Perhaps, someone somewhere has a diary record which would go some way to cast light on some of the 'who did what' mysteries. But there is no doubt that the 'Charlie Katz cash payment plan' inadvertently limited the need for what might, by now, be an impressive archive.

Bobby was always aware of the power that Charlie Katz and his equally fearsome wife Nita, wielded.

"Many of the players felt a chill running down their spine when he rang; I did myself in the early days. When Charlie spoke you reacted, and quickly. When Charlie was acting as the fixer he set himself aside from his musical role and became this tough Jewish businessman. He would ring up with a session booking but if you asked who the producer or arranger were he would say "Bobby please don't ask for the names of the higher ups." I found this hilarious in a sense but I didn't like it. There were obviously some producers and arrangers that I preferred to work for so I didn't think it unreasonable to ask who I would be working with."

Bobby remembers an early session recording with Eddy Mitchell for Disc Barclay in London. Charlie Katz was not only the fixer for the session but was also leading the string section of the orchestra on some rock'n'roll recordings. After the session Charlie paid the musicians their wages and then made his way to the control box. The one way sound system was still switched on so the musicians were able to hear the conversation in the control box. Charlie Katz was leaning with his back to the studio. He said to Jean Fernandez the musical director "I hope you were happy with the musicians. You know I always supply the best." Jean Fernandez said he was very happy and then added "I have got the cash for the session. You had better check that it is correct." Charlie took a wad of notes but, in his ingratiating way, said "Jean, please, please if I can't trust you who can I trust." Meanwhile he was holding the wad of notes behind his back skilfully counting them and checking that he had the right amount.

Clem Cattini, one of the UK's other major session drummers recalls an episode with Charlie Katz: "We were doing a session at the CBS Studios and the guitarist Roland Harker had not turned up. I had earphones on and could hear Charlie Katz in the control room saying to the producer "When one of my musicians does this I cross him out of the book. So far as I am concerned Roland Harker is dead." The unfortunate thing is that the reason Roland wasn't there is that he really was dead. He had died the night before."

One of Bobby's last studio dealings with Charlie Katz may provide an insight into the man's psyche. They were doing a session at Decca and for some reason that Bobby cannot now recollect, he got very angry with the musical director. Such was Bobby's occasional lack of control that he simply threw his drum sticks at the musical director and stormed out of the studio. This was wholly unacceptable behaviour whoever you were or however well you played. Charlie Katz, who was leading the strings at the session, chased out after Bobby, still with his violin under his chin. He shouted "Bobby, Bobby, stop, stop I need to talk to you immediately." Bobby stopped in the corridor and was conscious that all of the other members of the rhythm section were drifting into the corridor to see the rest of the cabaret.

"It was as though Charlie had a script prepared he was so fluent. He said "Bobby you have just committed the most terrible sin. You have thrown your drum sticks at the

Musical Director. I cannot and will not tolerate such behaviour. I believe this will now herald the end of your career. You will never work again, certainly not for me and I doubt for any other record company." "

By now he had Bobby by the collar even though Bobby was a good deal bigger. Bobby was trying to speak but was not being allowed to. "In the end I shouted "Charlie will you just shut your mouth for a moment." This brought a big "OOOHHH" from the rhythm section who thought now I was really in trouble. I told him in no uncertain terms what I thought of him and how I had always disliked him. I had great pleasure in telling him that I was getting out of the sessions and that I had accepted a job with Disc Barclay. I explained that I was going be starting my own production company producing records for Disc Barclay in England. His response was incredible. His demeanour changed completely. His fierce look disappeared and he put his arm around me saying "Well Bobby, you are going to need musicians for your sessions. You know where to come; we always get the best for everybody and for you I am sure I will be able to do a special deal." "

The consensus amongst those whose paths crossed with Charlie Katz, including those who crossed swords with him too, is that he was one of the truly great characters of the music industry. He was not universally liked but he was universally respected and he made a singular contribution to the session music industry of the 1960s. He has left a considerable musical legacy and his name is forever marked on some great music.

Bobby Becomes
a Session Player

The transition from Bobby Graham as a touring group drummer to being, virtually, a full-time session drummer was not planned; it is simply the way things turned out. Although Bobby had, in effect, been a session drummer in his days with The Outlaws, recording for Joe Meek, that was different from full-time disciplined session work.

"People very often ask me what was the first session that I ever did and to be truthful I can't honestly remember. Although I had done a lot of recording it was not what you would call session work. The actual title of the very first session that I ever attended I really can't remember. I think, but I may be wrong, that it was a thing by the Vernons Girls, conducted and arranged by Mike Leander, a young, up-and-coming, musician and arranger. Mike had heard me playing with Joe Brown and asked me to come along and do the session with him. Because, at the time, I couldn't read I had to go to Mike's office in Denmark Street and sit with him whilst he wrote the drum part out and explained it all to me so that I would be ready when I walked in on the session."

How, though, did it happen that Bobby was available for session work? The answer is that he and many other aspiring musicians spent a lot of time, when they were not on tour, in Denmark Street, London's Tin Pan Alley. This was where musicians and music publishers would meet. There were two venues that acted as magnets for those involved in the music industry. The first was a little coffee bar, the other was a pub. Both were busy.

"We'd just sit and talk about music and see who was doing what, who'd got all the work and who hadn't. A lot of arrangers and record company guys used to come along to the pub to drink down there. You started chatting with them and then you got your session work. That's how it really happened for me. I think I was in the Gioconda Coffee Bar when Mike Leander came in, came over to me and asked me if I'd like to come along to his session with The Vernons Girls. I agreed and, I think, that's how the session work started."

Bobby Graham had by now espoused the rock'n'roll and pop music concept; although his first love had been jazz he was very comfortable with the new genres. He is very quick to ensure that history records his great admiration for other drummers but reality demands that a context should be placed on his role at the time. "The word very quickly got around that there was this new drummer in town who had a totally different feel and technique from the normal session men. Don't get me wrong I'm not putting my colleagues down in any way whatsoever. My hero and mentor was Ronnie Verrall and I was and remain a massive fan of Kenny Clare. They both did sessions but they had been brought up through a jazz period. They were both brilliant drummers but they were big band drummers. Ronnie was with The Ted Heath Orchestra and Kenny was with The Johnny Dankworth Orchestra. A lot of what I played, I'd copied from them and then added my own feel and things to it. They were not really grounded in rock'n'roll. They didn't really care too much for it as music. So when I came in I had a totally new and different feel."

Record producers were keen to use Bobby Graham. "It wasn't just me. It was exactly the same with Jimmy Page. He again couldn't read but had this wonderful feel that very few of the English session guitarists could match. The same thing, of course, with Big Jim Sullivan, and so finally there became a little team of us that did many, many of the sessions of that day. I nicknamed our rhythm section The Musical Stuntmen because we used to do all the dangerous bits for the artists; like playing the right chords and playing the right beats in the right place."

The Musical Stuntmen were a very able group. "I could not believe I was playing with such fantastically talented musicians." It is invidious to ask who they all were because, almost inevitably, someone will be left out of the dramatis personae. In no particular order Bobby remembers with great affection the real stars of the session scene: "Vic Flick was one of the regular rhythm section guys on most of the major sessions and when I first came on the session scene he was one of the few people to really go out of his way to help and encourage me."

His haunting guitar sound is the trade mark of the James Bond films, and it must make him feel very proud to know that his playing on that theme alone has probably been heard by billions of people. His world famous sound was achieved by using a Clifford Essex Paragon cello bodied F hole guitar fitted with a DeArmond volume pedal into a Vox 15 watt amplifier, the orchestra was recorded in one pass – no 48 track recording then. Vic is a composer and arranger and now lives in Santa Monica, California.

"Big Jim Sullivan is held in the highest esteem by both old and especially new guitar players; he is a giant amongst session men and has probably been on more recordings in his life than any other guitarist. His versatility is just amazing." Big Jim Sullivan features throughout the story of Bobby Graham's recordings

"Jimmy Page came into the session scene in the early 1960s and had an immediate impact. He changed the whole approach to guitar playing. In those days the established guitarists always played 'written' solos. They were often played, without much 'feel' or even enthusiasm. Jimmy changed all that, possibly because at that time he didn't read at all and he had that hard screaming sound that was so 'in' at that time. He and Big Jim were brilliant together; Big Jim was more precise but Jimmy had this wonderful dirty sound."

"I have only happy memories of Eric Ford. He was a dear friend who is sadly no longer with us. Eric was another young guitarist who got into session work in a big way, he also doubled on bass guitar and was one of the first six string bass players in the country. He played on loads of sessions; I particularly remember him on many of The Dave Clark Five recordings."

"Brian Daley was one of the more established players on the circuits and is a big but gentle man. We nicknamed him 'Banana Fingers Daley' because he had really big fingers for a guitarist, but he made wonderful music with those old fat fingers." He later went on to write and play the music for *Postman Pat,* the children's series.

Another player who attracted Bobby's admiration was Joe Morretti. "Joe was a Scotsman. He was a great guitarist. He played that fantastic guitar solo on 'Shakin All Over' by Johnny Kidd and The Pirates, and he soon became one of our busiest session guitarists."

"Alan Weighell was one of the most-used bass guitar players on the sessions. In fact, I can't believe there was any bass guitarist who played on more sessions than Alan. He started his professional career with Tommy Steele and The Steele Men; he had a prolific career as a fine musician. He is a very quiet unassuming man, and I always knew it would be a good session if Alan was on bass/bass guitar as he was a really good solid player."

"Brian Brocklehurst is a real unsung hero. All the years that I knew 'Brock' I never saw him turn up at sessions in a car, I don't think the man could even drive. He would travel from studio to studio by bike, with the bass amp in a specially built basket on the front and a huge double bass strapped to his back. He would precariously wobble his way to sessions through the rush hour traffic always with his 'Sherlock Holmes' pipe unlit in his mouth. He was a terrific player; nothing ever fazed him."

"Clem Cattini is one of my very close friends in the music industry, I first met Clem as a touring musician when he was with Johnny Kidd and The Pirates and, of course, later when he led The Tornadoes who had the worldwide hit with 'Telstar'." Clem went on to become one of the key players on the session scene and like Bobby has played on hundreds of records. "I have a lot of respect for Clem both as a drummer and as a friend."

"Ronnie Verrall was my all time hero, he came from a big band jazz background – The Ted Heath Orchestra and The Jack Parnell Band. It is no exaggeration to say that Ronnie Verrall's playing was one of the reasons that I decided to become a drummer. His playing was just superb. He also ghosted for Animal on *The Muppet Show*. He was truly one of the great and inspiring characters of the Music Industry."

"Stan Barrett was the number one tuned percussionist on recording sessions, TV shows and radio broadcasts. I think he had had formal musical training in the military. He was a first class reader of music and played an enormous range of instruments including vibes, glockenspiel, tympani, tubular bells and Latin percussion instruments. Stan was, and still is, one of my great mates in the industry, he is a true gentlemen and looked after me like a father in those long gone days."

Apologies are due to those whose names are not included; it is not intentional.

So we have set the scene.

A Typical Day

Of course, there was no such thing as a typical day. There were, though, many days with a similar pattern. No two days were ever quite the same.

Although almost exclusively London-based, it was, nonetheless, a peripatetic existence: every day as he struggled with his drum kit, Bobby was conscious of the fact that, with the possible exception of the tuned percussionist, his was the most physically demanding of the session players in terms of transporting the kit. He travelled between recording studios always having to carry his full kit with him; even in those days the kit could never be left in the car during the day or overnight so was loaded and unloaded several times a day.

"In fact there were some days that I wished I had picked the harmonica as my chosen instrument."

What follows is what, to Bobby, became an unexceptional day; the epithet 'ordinary' could never be applied to it.

6.30am	Out of bed at his home in Chingford in anticipation of setting off for the first session of the day at the Pye Studios at Bryanston Street.
7.00am	Load up the drum kit into the car and start the journey through the rush hour traffic.
9.00am	Arrive at Bryanston Street; find that there is nowhere to park, all the meters full. Hurriedly unload the kit and carry it down to the studio. No roadies for the session men so it was 'do it yourself'. Rush back to the car and drive to an indoor car park. Run back to the studio to set the kit up before the session starts.

10.00am   A big session with The Tony Hatch Orchestra. This one has a large string section (the gentlemen) and the rhythm section (the ruffians). A productive but hard session, taking the full three hours with a very short coffee break.

1.00pm   Finish the session at Pye. Dismantle the kit. Run to get the car. Double park outside the studio. Hump the drums up from the studio and load them into the car. There is one hour to get to the EMI studios at Abbey Road, and have the kit set up ready. So no lunch but get there just in time. Parking no problem. All ready by 2.00pm. Interesting session with PJ Proby and Charles Blackwell. Overrun on studio time but finish at 5.30 with everyone happy with the session.

5.30pm   There is now an hour and a half to get to the Decca Studios in West Hampstead for the first of two evening sessions. Get to the studio and park. Rush to the local pub to grab a sandwich and a beer before heading back to the studio to set the kit up. Another busy session, this one with Them. The session has other session players, Jimmy Page, Big Jim Sullivan and Alan Weighell. The producer for the session is American Bert Berns. Another good session producing four tracks in three hours. The other players leave to go home or, more probably, the pub. Bobby stays to do another session to overdub some drums on some Brian Poole tracks. His producer, Mike Smith arrives late and so the session does not start until 11.15pm.

12.45am   The session ends and so it's time to pack the kit into the car for the fourth time that day (with the same number of unloads) and then drive home. Unload the car again. Into bed at 2.30

and as soon as the head hits the pillow, the alarm rings and it's 6.30 and time to get up for another day.

Whilst loading the car a neighbour comments "What a glamorous life you boys have."

The Sessions

Having looked at a session and the role of the Fixer we need to see what role the session player really had in the popular music of the sixties. No-one with an informed mind could ever doubt that the contribution made by session musicians in that era is immense.

Contemporary recognition of the phenomenon that was 'the session player' was, though, distinctly limited. It has rarely been advertised by those that benefited from the skill of others who were, and largely remain anonymous and unacknowledged.

How far did our knowledge of the role of the session musician extend during the sixties? In truth, for most ordinary music fans, it was probably confined to the most publicised, and understandably most spectacular example: namely, that Ringo Starr did not play on the first Beatles' single 'Love Me Do.' Although this was not exactly advertised at the time, word soon got out and, to Ringo and the other Beatles' credit, it was never denied. It is especially interesting because this was the only time in the whole of their recording career that one of the four was stood down for a recording. That this was made known four decades ago explains why this undoubted truth has given rise to a variety of stories; some of which at least stretch the limits of credulity.

There are several reasons why Ringo was not used on this track; none of them remarkable in themselves and all were typical of the time. The Beatles' still-latent talent was not even obvious to George Martin (as he then was) who produced their first, and almost all, later recordings.

In January 1962 Martin heard a demo tape that The Beatles had recorded. He thought it was "absolutely awful" but, as a favour to their young manager, Brian Epstein, he agreed to give them an hour of studio time. He did not know at that time that, according to him "they had been turned down by virtually every other label and every other recording person in the country." Had he known that, George Martin might not even have given them the limited opportunity he did.

However, when he heard them play at the EMI studios he was captivated by their natural verve and contagious enthusiasm. It was, though, blindingly obvious that they had virtually no studio experience. What really knocked him out was their personality and charisma. The three front men, John, Paul and George worked well together. He was much less impressed with the drummer, Pete Best. Although, in George Martin's view, he was the best looking of the group he was conspicuously quiet; he definitely did not have the personality of the other three. He was a reasonably proficient drummer but he was not what George Martin called "top notch".

After the first session two momentous things happened: firstly, George Martin signed the group to Parlophone, (EMI's sister label) on a very 'mean' contract. Secondly, after George Martin voiced his concerns about Pete Best to Epstein, Pete's time as a Beatle came to an end.

So, by the time of the next recording session Pete Best had been replaced as The Beatles' drummer by Ringo Starr, he having been enticed from another popular Liverpool group Rory Storm and The Hurricanes. It was not necessarily for his drumming that Ringo was chosen; he, too, was a charismatic character who made an easy fit with the other three. He had no studio experience and so when The Fab Four, as they were soon to be known, arrived to record their *Please Please Me* album, George Martin took control. The decision was taken as to which track would be released as The Beatles' first single: it was to be 'Love Me Do.' George Martin decided that Andy

White, a highly-experienced session drummer, should play drums on the track and he did. History records that a twelve track LP was recorded in a twelve hour session. Ringo Starr played on the other tracks.

George Martin rationalised it to Brian Epstein by saying "I don't care what you do with them as a group ... from a purely sound point of view I will get someone in for the recording session."

Cost was a major influence; studio time was expensive and limited to whichever slot as could be booked. There simply was no time or money available for musicians to hone their studio skills. This truth is universally acknowledged; interestingly the extensive use of studio or session musicians was not then the subject of much public interest. Apart from the overall sound, the most important thing was the physical appearance of the group or singer. Millions swooned without any idea if their idol could play or not.

What is the relevance of all of this to Bobby? It is twofold. Firstly, in June 1962 when Bobby was playing with Joe Brown and The Bruvvers, they played two gigs in Liverpool; one at the Cavern Club and the other at Litherland Town Hall. After the second gig most members of the group went to a club called the Blue Angel. There, Brian Epstein sought out Bobby Graham and confided in him that he was very happy with a group he was managing called The Beatles. He saw a considerable future for them. He went on to explain that there was a problem; he was not happy with the drummer, Pete Best. (It is unclear as to whether this was as the result of Brian Epstein's conversation with George Martin or wholly independent of it.) Epstein claimed he was having trouble with Pete Best's mother and so he had decided to oust Pete Best and get a new drummer. The way he spoke left Bobby in no doubt that he was being offered the job.

"I wasn't interested. I was playing with a great outfit and already hitting the charts. I said to Brian "Why would

I want to join a group in Liverpool that nobody's ever heard of?" "

The matter was taken no further and Bobby stayed with Joe Brown and The Bruvvers. Brian Epstein did find a new drummer. Within months everybody had heard of The Beatles and the rest as they say...

Many, indeed most, would expect Bobby Graham to suffer at least a tinge of regret at this missed opportunity. It seems not; Bobby is entirely sanguine about the whole affair. "I don't think the drumming would have been a problem. The thing is that one of the outstanding features that made The Beatles was the fact that they were four mop topped lads from Liverpool. It was a big part of their image. Somehow I can't see that it would have been quite the same if it had been three Scousers with mop tops and one geezer with a carrot topped, slash back hairstyle from North London. It doesn't have the same feel to it."

Secondly, it provides a vivid example of how the use of session players could facilitate a group's introduction to recording.

Bobby got into session playing thanks to his skill and versatility. He did not read music; there may be a perception that drummers, especially 'pop music' drummers do not read music. In fact, session players of any instrument were generally expected not only to read music but to sight read. However, as the days of the sixties session musicians dawned, this essential pre-requisite clashed with reality and the mandatory requirement of sight reading diminished. The electric guitar and rock'n'roll saw to that.

For example, the electric bass guitar was a relatively recent invention and a still more recent import into the United Kingdom. Although a number of players converted from the string (or double) bass, many who took up the instrument had no musical training, history or knowledge. Many, indeed most, six string guitarists were similarly self-taught, although a lot of them may have benefited from basic training from books such as Bert Weedon's *Play in a Day*. Most learned as they practised and played, often replicating the sounds heard on American imported blues records. Jimmy Page is a good example. He is undoubtedly one of the greatest session guitarists of the period. He later became a hugely successful recording artist as a founding member of Led Zeppelin and later still in his own right. To begin with, Page could not read music. Yet he features on a vast number of studio sessions and has graced a colossal number of tracks with his virtuoso skills. In fact, he did learn to read music and how that happened is a story worth telling.

One of the greatest guitarists the UK has produced is Big Jim Sullivan. Having been an original member of Marty Wilde's Wildcats, his cv thereafter makes fascinating reading. He was a teenage prodigy who was playing on sessions before his eighteenth birthday. He was self-taught and when he hit the big time, could not read music. He still remembers the day when his musical knowledge let him down: "We were booked to play at Elstree. I was given a lift there by Judd Proctor who was another guitarist on the session. The producer was Stanley Black. There was a seventy piece orchestra there. We were given music but it was meaningless to me although I didn't let on. After a while the producer announced over the tannoy "would the third guitarist pack up his guitar and go." I was kicked off the session. It was pretty humiliating. Judd Proctor gave me a lift home and he gave me some very good advice: "Get all the music you can and study it. Anything, Mozart, Bach, Cantatas, anything. So I did. Six months later I could sight read perfectly. Years later when Jimmy Page was struggling at a session I told him I would teach him and so I did."

Bobby Graham had similar experiences. Drummers, too, were meant to be able to read. He could not. He found himself booked into the wrong studio, Decca 3, playing with a seventy piece orchestra while Kenny Clare, a perfect sight reader was in an adjoining studio playing rock'n'roll.

On the session Andy White was playing drums and Bobby, unusually, was playing the tenor drum. Bobby failed to come in on time when the recording started but, happily for him, the conductor was a former drummer, Bobby Williams. He spotted the problem and called a break in recording. He pointed out to Bobby that the tune was a military march and Bobby was happy and completed the session. "It was really scary."

So session work was not going to be easy.

The Dave Clark Five

One of the most frequently asked questions about 1960s music is "Did Dave Clark play the drums on the group's hit records?" The supplementary question is "If he didn't, who did?" The answers, though deliberately obfuscated, are, in fact, brutally simple: "No he did not. It was Bobby Graham." It was Bobby Graham who played the distinctive drum beat on the first and many more of The Dave Clark Five's hit records. Bobby continued to play with Dave Clark up until 1967.

These questions and answers beg many more. In order to put the answers in perspective we need to look back at the career of The Dave Clark Five.

According to contemporary publicity material Dave Clark was born in North London in 1942. From childhood his was always a strong personality and he had a driving ambition. To those that knew him it came as no surprise that he found his way into films, initially as an extra. This began when he was still in his teens. He featured in a large number of, mostly low budget, British films although, by the nature of the work, he was not credited with any of the roles he played.

From a child he was, apparently, a dedicated Tottenham Hotspur fan, supporting them in their glory years and sticking with them during less successful times. He was a keen and skilful player himself; he played full back for a local youth club team. When the team wanted to go on a playing tour to Holland it was the resourceful Dave Clark who had the inspirational idea of forming a group with the laudable ambition of helping his team raise the necessary finance for the trip. It was a portend of the financial acumen he developed and has retained.

Dave Clark had had no musical training and played no instrument. He bought a set of drums for £10 and determined to become a drummer.

Accounts vary as to the true genesis of The Dave Clark Five. What is reasonably clear is that the original scheme was that the group should be a backing group for Stan Saxon who had sought to establish himself as a singer in North London. Other accounts suggest that Stan Saxon joined the group after they had been formed. Initially, there was an obvious skiffle influence in the group's sound. Two early members of the group, Chris Wells and Mick Ryan proved transient but then the group formed as an autonomous unit with Dave Clark on drums, Mike Smith on vocals and keyboard, Lenny Davidson on lead guitar, Rick Huxley playing bass guitar and Denis Payton on saxophone.

They found plenty of gigs in the local area, not just because of their fundraising image but because they were a charismatic outfit, Dave Clark had an extrovert and engaging stage personality. They soon extended their sphere of operation and began to play at American forces bases.

Their music evolved to meet the popular interest of the day and they found themselves making a demo tape of dance band music for the Mecca theatre organisation.

By the end of the 1950s their ambitions had expanded still further and they determined the time to be right to seek a record deal. In 1960 they struck lucky and signed with Pye's sister label Ember. Their recording career began. They released three singles which did not sell. They then recorded on the Columbia label. Their first release on Columbia was 'Mulberry Bush' which was a rock interpretation of the nursery rhyme. It did nothing for The Dave Clark Five although, interestingly, in a slightly different version, it was a top ten hit for Traffic five years later, as the theme song of the film of almost the same name. Many note that Steve Winwood's vocals sounded not much different from Mike Smith's.

The Dave Clark Five then released a cover version of 'Do You Love Me' which was also released on Columbia Records. This had been a major hit in the United States for a Tamla Motown group called The Contours. It was commonplace to cover US hits because the music often did not achieve transatlantic success, not for any particular reason, but the sound was sometimes a little alien and capable of a more familiar interpretation. Unfortunately, another producer had spotted the potential of the song and recorded a version by Brian Poole and The Tremeloes. This latter version entered the charts in July 1963 and made Number 1. The Dave Clark Five version made it to Number 30. Ironically, this proved to be the apogee of Brian Poole's career but the beginning of huge success for The Dave Clark Five. In fact Bobby Graham played on the recording of 'Do You Love Me' but purely as a session player with no specific artistic role: he simply played the drum part in replica of The Contours' version

However, there was nothing about The Dave Clark Five sound which was unique or even distinctive. A new dimension was needed. Enter Bobby Graham under the inspirational and innovative production of Dave Clark: things changed. Bobby already had an excellent reputation as a brilliant stage and studio drummer. He was in great demand as a session player. He had met Dave Clark when Dave Clark had decided he needed to polish his drumming in order to play in the recording studio, which was a wholly different situation from playing modest live gigs. He went to Bobby's Chingford flat to refine his playing skills.

Dave Clark was anxious to produce the group's records, something he did with great success. The dual role of producer and drummer was expecting too much: "he decided he could not be in the studio, as the drummer, and in the control box upstairs as the producer, so he called me in to play on the sessions."

Dave Clark went on to produce the records, although many claim that Mike Smith should at least be credited with equal status as producer. The production credits used pseudonyms.

Bobby recalls the session where 'Glad All Over' was recorded. It was at Columbia's Lansdowne Road Studios in London where a full day session was booked. The recording engineer on the session was Adrian Kerridge. On many of The Dave Clark Five's recordings the musical arranger was the legendary Les Reed. Bobby was not the only session player on the recording: Eric Ford played bass guitar.

After initial rehearsal the players were set for a run through of the main track. Bobby played a driving beat which he did not regard as out of the ordinary. Dave Clark's voice came from the production suite saying "Bob, could you play it simpler, I might have to mime this on TV in a couple of weeks." This light hearted banter was instrumental in creating the sound which everyone associates with the Dave Clark sound. Bobby played a simpler version but was greeted with an even more plaintive cry: Bobby said "Dave, all I can do is play everything four to the bar."

Bobby played 'the flam beat' both hands and feet pounding on the whole kit. Dave Clark was delighted not merely with its simplicity but also the sound it made. "That was how it started – though the sound that was created was enhanced by the overdubbing of stamping on the studio floorboards." It was clear by the end of the session that a novel sound had been recorded. Although the stomping drum beat is defining, the strength of Mike Smith's vocals is not to be underestimated.

'Glad All Over', which had been written by Dave Clark and Mike Smith, was quickly released on the Columbia label and entered the charts in November of 1963. By January of the following year it had knocked The Beatles' 'I Want To Hold Your Hand' off the top spot and was in the charts for a total of nineteen weeks.

As was commonplace a follow-up single was swiftly

recorded which closely replicated the individual sound of the precursor. 'Bits and Pieces' was recorded with the same line-up at the same studio and Bobby's driving drum playing was an important part of the sound. The record entered the charts in February 1964, overlapping with 'Glad All Over', went to Number 2 in the charts and stayed in the charts for eleven weeks.

Bobby Graham went on to play on the great majority of The Dave Clark Five's recordings until 1967. Although their first top ten singles provide the definitive sound, the group continued to enjoy success until they disbanded in 1970. They enjoyed spectacular success in the United States, for a while rivalling The Beatles on that side of the Atlantic.

Bobby is entirely sanguine about this chapter in his recording career. He does not complain that he was not credited with playing on these hit singles.

"I was doing what I was paid to do and I was enjoying myself. If they got to Number 1 in the charts, then good luck to them. What people don't realise is that I got paid if they got to Number 1 and I still got paid even if the track was never released. True, session players would have been better off if we had been on a share of the royalties on successful songs but that was never an option."

In fact, the early financial acumen shown by Dave Clark was such that, from the start, he ensured that he owned the copyright of all the masters of the songs the group played. Later he bought all the black & white archives of the *Ready, Steady, Go* television shows and other pieces of musical history. He has deservedly done well as the result.

The final question frequently asked is: "If Dave Clark didn't play on the studio recordings then how did he manage on stage and in television studio settings?" That, of course, is another story. To the curious, scrutiny of contemporary archive footage may go a long way to answering this perceptive question.

PJ Proby

During the 1960s Bobby Graham recorded with, literally, hundreds of groups and singers. He finds it invidious to rank them in any order of preference although he enjoyed some sessions much more than others. Some have left an indelible impression on his memory.

"One of my favourite ever artists was PJ Proby. He was fantastic fun, a great singer and a wonderful showman. He was one of the few who was really grateful for the contribution we made. We had a lot of fun together."

PJ Proby, was born James Marcus Smith on the 6th of November 1938 in Houston, Texas. As a very young child he was influenced by the music that he heard in church. This was predominantly gospel singing at the Baptist Church he attended with his parents. As he grew, up he spent a lot of time singing in the clubs and bars of Houston and met and sang with Elvis Presley, Tommy Sands, Tennessee Ernie Ford, George Jones and many others.

From a young age he cherished the ambition of becoming a singer and songwriter but promised his parents that he would graduate from High School before embarking on such a career path. He kept his promise and attended, firstly, the San Marcos Military Academy in Texas and in 1957 he graduated from the Western Military Academy in Alton, Illinois. From there he made his way to Hollywood and made contact with his old friend Tommy Sands. Tommy introduced Jim Smith to one of the leading vocal coaches of the day, Lillian Goodman. She, in turn, introduced him to the Oscar-winning song writer Ray Gilbert. Both Goodman and Gilbert recognised the talent that Jim Smith had so he was then introduced to agents who had a proven track record. They signed Jim Smith with the comment "great voice, awfully ordinary name." So Jim Smith became Jett Powers.

At around the same time Jim, as he continues to be known, met Sharon Sheeley who was to have a profound effect upon his career. Sharon Sheeley had recently written the Ricky Nelson hit 'Poor Little Fool.' Ricky Nelson was a teenage radio and television star who had grown up in radio and television soaps before enjoying great success as a singer. In the 1950s and early 1960s he rivalled Elvis Presley and Pat Boone for record sales. He has the additional familial distinction of having a father (Ozzie) and twin sons (Gunnär and Matthew) who topped the US charts in (1935 and 1990 respectively). 'Poor Little Fool' topped the US charts in the summer of 1958 and reached Number 4 in the UK charts in August that year.

When Jim met Sharon she was the girlfriend of Eddie Cochran. Jim became friendly with this circle and began going out with Sharon Sheeley's friend Dotty Harmony. He began to collaborate in songwriting and also, briefly, sang with The Hollywood Argyles who scored a major hit in 1960 with 'Alley Oop' reaching Number 1 in the United States and Number 24 in the UK. It was a novelty song and the group's only chart success.

Sharon Sheeley then took Jim to Liberty Records who signed him on a singing and songwriting contract. Although a great stride forward, the exclusive terms of the contract proved troublesome in later years. Of greater impact was the fact that Sharon persuaded Jim to change his name for a second time; she chose the name of a boy she had dated in Junior High School and so Jett Powers became PJ Proby.

PJ Proby recorded 'Try To Forget Her' and 'There Stands The One' with vocal backing by The Johnny Mann Singers. A young Glenn Campbell was on guitar and Hal Blaine on drums. The record was not a particular success, due, in part to the lack of marketing or radio exposure. He then recorded a Sharon Sheeley and Jackie de Shannon song 'The Other Side Of Town' and a Dick Glasser composition 'Watch Me Walk Away' as the B side. Again, no particular promotion was mounted and, again, no great success was achieved even though the production was very good.

PJ Proby was extensively used as a session singer doing backing vocals for many of the great artists of the day, including BB King, Johnny Cash, Little Richard and Elvis Presley. Many might have thought that this should have been enough but Jim craved a solo career. It came about in a slightly curious way.

Sharon Sheeley and Jackie de Shannon were very well connected in the music industry and knew Jack Good. Books have been written about Jack Good; for present purposes it is sufficient to say that he was a hugely influential record producer and then television producer.

By 1963 popular music was changing; the emergence of the British influence was still in its early stages but the crescendo had begun. The Beatles were becoming a major influence and their manager, Brian Epstein, was anxious to exploit their commercial potential. He invited, or persuaded, Jack Good to produce a television special for a worldwide audience to be called *Around The Beatles*. As the name implies it was to showcase talent associated with The Fab Four. Jack Good brought some PJ Proby demo tapes and played them to Brian Epstein.

This was enough. PJ Proby was summoned to London and the show was broadcast around the world, courtesy of the new Telstar Satellite. The impact of the show, for all those appearing on it, was outstanding.

Partly as the result of the programme, Jack Good was able to broker a recording deal for PJ Proby with Decca records. It was arranged that a top set of, mostly session, players should assemble for the first recording session. Listening to the product of that session makes it easy to see the quality of those assembled.

Bobby aged 17 in 1957

Bobby Graham and Johnny Sawyer during their epic drum battle on the classic 'Skin Deep" in 1960 playing the Empire Theatre, Butlins, Filey in Yorkshire

The Big Band Sound of the Teddy Foster Orchestra; Bobby smiling and adjusting his tie

Rock and Roll with Reg Hawkins, Billy Gray, Danny Rivers and Bobby Graham in 1961 at Filey

In action with Joe Brown and The Bruvvers, 1962

And relaxing backstage

1962: publicity photo taken by Carlton Drums at the launch of the
'Bobby Graham Giant Kit' and (below) press advert featuring the
headline 'Top Stars play Carlton'

Ember Records launch reception, 1963: Bobby Graham and John Barry stand in front of a blow-up photo of Bobby

Bobby and Jazz singer Annie Ross

Decca Studios, West Hampstead, 1964: recording engineer Terry
Johnson and Bobby Graham

The John Barry Seven under the direction of Bobby Graham in 1965

Bobby circa 1978

Bobby at home with son Shawn and wife Belinda

Session times were set to very clear timetables, something that PJ Proby knew from his many session recordings in the States. This first session was set for 10.00am, which was recognised to be a reasonable time even in the hedonistic 60s. The musicians were there and Bobby Graham had his kit finely tuned. It was a case of *Hamlet* without the Prince. Time marched on and a series of increasingly frantic phone calls were made. Several times the point has been made that technology was different then: there were no mobile phones. Attempts to contact our artist were unsuccessful. The phone at the flat he was thought to be renting went unanswered. The musicians drank coffee, became bored and contemplated an empty day.

At about 12.50, just before ten to one, the doors of the studio were flung open and PJ Proby arrived, with his considerable entourage. He was one of the first to accumulate such an entourage which was, at least superficially, impressive. He had his own hairdresser who moved with him, even to the studio. Others had less defined roles but acted as though they were an essential accoutrement: all this before PJ Proby had achieved any tangible success. Others might have construed this as a gesture of arrogance but to Bobby Graham this was more a reflection of PJ Proby's extravagant personality. It seems to have caused offence to no-one.

Jack Good was unimpressed by this tardy arrival and went into what Bobby calls "a big one"; he regaled PJ Proby with the problems that had been created by committing the studio and a big team of musicians to an empty session. PJ was understanding, conciliatory and disarming. He said "What's the problem Jack. You told me the session was ten to one. I make it ten to one. I'm here. Lets go."

Go they did. In the course of the session they recorded two fantastic tracks 'Hold Me' which was a major hit in 1964, reaching Number 3 in the charts in May of that year and 'Together' which reached Number 8 in the charts less than four months later.

Bobby recalls the session. It was the usual team of musical heavyweights: Jimmy Page and Big Jim Sullivan on guitar, Arthur Greenslade on piano and Alan Weighell on bass. The session, at the IBC Studios in London, was exhilarating, once it began. Bobby remembers PJ moving into the vocal booth. "It was fantastic from the start. When you get a great singer like that, with so much feeling in his voice, you just go with the flow. We thundered into the arrangement that Charles Blackwell had written and it was just sensational. The whole thing gelled together and I think we put the whole track [Hold Me] down in two takes, maybe three."

Charles Blackwell also found the process very enjoyable: "Once we got started it went very well. Jim Proby has a very distinctive voice. He listened to what I told him and he performed very well. Having Bobby and the others playing made it a lot easier, of course, but fair play to Jim, he was very good."

It was the same with 'Together'; two or three takes and it was done. Not only was the session hugely enjoyable but the late arrival of the artist meant that the session players earned some welcome overtime.

PJ Proby seems also to have enjoyed the proceedings. He has a vivid recall although not every detail accords with others' recollection: "It was pouring with rain on a bleak and stormy afternoon in 1964 when, soaking wet, I stumbled through the doors of a little studio called IBC in London for a rushed recording session set up by close friend and mentor, the legendary Jack Good. Immediately, he guided me around the floor to meet the little band of musicians he had called in. "PJ this is your drummer Bobby Graham, you're gonna love him dear boy; he's Hal Blaine, Jerry Allison and Sandy Nelson all rolled into one." Well Jack was right. Bob took me through the session like I had never left Hollywood. Gave me a beat that put me in the charts at Number 3 and continued to give birth to my rhythms on countless recordings throughout the sixties, hit after hit. Thank you Bobby. Thank you friend."

Bobby next worked with PJ Proby on his album *I Am PJ Proby*. This, too, was recorded at the Decca Studios in West Hampstead. The album was very successful. By the time of its recording Jim Proby's reputation for poor timekeeping was well known. At each session the musicians contrived a sweepstake as to the time that the star would arrive. They each paid £1 and then estimated the time of Jim's arrival. The person with the closest estimate won. After a few sessions, PJ learned of the scheme. He sent one of his entourage to the session; he entered the sweepstake and predicted a remarkably early arrival time. PJ Proby arrived to the second of the time forecast by his 'plant', early for a session for the only time in anyone's recollection. He scooped the pool but had the good grace to invite everyone for a drink afterwards.

Contractual problems then arose for PJ Proby. He was still signed to Liberty and in fundamental breach of a very tight contract. Liberty enforced the agreement, causing problems for the artist, but this is not the place to recite the details.

PJ Proby's visual presence was probably unique; he wore his hair in a ponytail, which was innovative even in the days of increasingly long hair. He had a great future in prospect but what many still believe to have been a publicity stunt went horribly wrong. On the 29th of January 1965 PJ Proby was appearing on stage at the Fairfield Hall, Croydon. He was playing to a sell out audience, when his bell bottomed velvet trousers split in the area of the groin. It caused a sensation. The press interest was intense and called for an explanation. PJ Proby was superficially convincing in explaining that the 'accident' was the result of a deficiency in the strength of the fabric of the trousers. He might have got away with it but for the fact that two days later the same thing happened.

Although this led to a widely enthusiastic reception from the audience this did not result in general public approbation. Even though history records the 60s as being a period of sexual liberation and a great loosening of the perception of morality, there was still at the time a strong undercurrent of propriety that could easily be offended. The redoubtable Mary Whitehouse was at the vanguard of his critics and made several meals of the incident.

Was it an accident and was the second 'accident' a coincidence. PJ Proby sums it up in a short rhetorical question: "Do you set fire to your money? If I had known the effect this was going to have on my career I would have gone on stage in a suit of armour."

The response to the incident was surprisingly hostile and many believe it was a seminal moment in Jim Proby's career. He never really recovered his reputation in the UK although his package concert tours sell out wherever he goes. In the month following the incident Liberty released an appropriately titled single 'I Apologise' which reached Number 11 in the charts.

His chart success in 1964 had included another top ten hit with 'Somewhere' and continued with 'Maria,' which reached Number 8 in November 1965, but after that he never had another top ten hit. Bobby Graham thinks this a great pity. "He was a very talented guy with a really big voice; he was great to work with and I liked him a lot."

This chapter is mostly about PJ Proby; Bobby is more than happy to acknowledge that his involvement with PJ was only one chapter in an interesting career for the artist. However, the driving influence in the most influential session which PJ Proby ever recorded relied upon the precision playing of the session musicians who augmented his great voice. Listen again to 'Hold Me' and 'Together;' although the voice is dominant the musical accompaniment is outstanding. Bobby is pleased and proud to have been part of this episode in musical history.

Some Fantastic Ladies

Some of the greatest sessions on which Bobby played were with female singers. Individually and collectively they enjoyed great chart success which, after all, was the principal aim of recording.

One of those that Bobby most enjoyed recording with was Dusty Springfield – "a favourite singer but not always my favourite person."

Dusty Springfield was born Mary O'Brien in London on the 16th of April 1939. She was brought up in a musical, but not always harmonious household. There was sibling rivalry, even before the phrase had been invented, between her and her elder brother Dion. She was convent-educated and astonished one of the nuns responsible for her care when, as a ten year old, she announced that she wanted to be a blues singer. Her father's extensive record collection and his fascination for the singing of Peggy Lee had had a profound influence upon his daughter.

Her first formal singing role was as a member of The Lana Sisters after responding to an advertisement for a third singer to join an established sister act. She learned a lot during her brief period as a member of this singing trio. From there she became a founder member of The Springfields, with two young men, one of whom was her brother Dion. Mary O'Brien became 'Dusty Springfield' and Dion became 'Tom Springfield.' They played and sang commercial folk music, got a recording contract and had five hits in the two years from the summer of 1961. Two of the five made Number 5 in the charts 'Island of Dreams' in December 1962 and 'Say I Won't Be There' in March 1963. Dusty became restless as the group struggled to preserve their identity as commercial folk singers as opposed to pop singers. Not only that but her's had shown through as the dominant personality and her voice cried out for solo treatment. Dusty left to pursue a solo career.

This started in the middle of 1963 and spanned the next four decades, admittedly with some long interludes between hits. Her trademark bouffant hair and heavy dark eye makeup made her's a very distinctive appearance. Her voice was rich and versatile confirming the prophecy she had made as a ten year old.

She could be very difficult. She suffered from mood swings which could take her from inappropriate euphoria to inexplicable troughs of depression in minutes, with no obvious catalyst. Bobby was playing on one session with her when she took against something he played; no question or query was directed towards the drums; instead a full cup of coffee was dispatched, which found its target. Her occasional tantrums earned her the nickname amongst the session players of 'Rusty Springboard'.

In contrast, she could be so charming and was so talented. Bobby recorded an album with her of which he remains extremely, and justly, proud. The album, *A Girl Called Dusty* enjoyed rapturous critical acclaim and put Dusty firmly on the map as a major player.

This, though, was not the first recording that Bobby did with Dusty, he also played on most of her singles; these began to hit the charts in November of 1963. 'I Only Want To Be With You' reached Number 4, 'Stay Awhile' Number 13 and 'I Just Don't Know What To Do With Myself' Number 3; all of this in a seven month time frame. She had fourteen more chart hits during the 1960s including her only Number 1. In March of 1966 she hit the top spot with 'You Don't Have To Say You Love Me.'

Bobby Graham remembers the recording of this Number 1 not because of any particular happening there but by the frank realisation at the end of the session that they had recorded something special.

Dusty was no great fan of singing in the studio setting. She found them not so much claustrophobic (though that as well) but felt that the soundproofing and wall cladding had the effect of deadening the nuances in her singing. She felt that this imposed an unacceptable restriction on her vocal repertoire. Some of the steps which were taken to enhance the sound and capture the subtleties of her voice Bobby found to be reminiscent of his days recording with Joe Meek at 304 Holloway Road.

On one occasion, when recording at the Phillips Records Studio in Stanhope Place, in London, a set of microphones were rigged up in the ladies lavatories; this created an echo and was much to the liking of Dusty Springfield. The recording went well and the product was very pleasing.

She was not a lady to spend time choosing her words to preserve the sensitivities of others. In modern parlance she was no respecter of individuals. Bobby found in time that he was not alone amongst drummers in incurring the wrath of Dusty Springfield. On an American Tour she had a falling out, on stage, with Buddy Rich, (generally acknowledged to have been the greatest drummer in the world; Bobby is certainly of this view). This display of rudeness by Dusty Springfield led to Buddy Rich storming off stage for the only time in his long and illustrious career. Dusty Springfield's contribution to British music history is phenomenal. Her versatility extended the parameters as recently as the nineties with her recording with The Pet Shop Boys. She seemed to glide easily into this new genre and attracted the approbation of all her old fans and made many new ones. Bobby was greatly saddened to hear of Dusty Springfield's death on the 2nd of March 1999: "she was a very special, very talented lady."

Another of those with whom Bobby Graham enjoyed recording was Kathy Kirby. Kathy had done a long apprenticeship before she found fame. She was a singer with The Bert Ambrose Orchestra for some years from the late 1950s. Bert Ambrose, who was four decades older than Kathy Kirby, became her manager and mentor.

Bobby remembers the relationship as being "a bit weird." He was not alone in forming this view. All of the session players noted the Svengali-like influence Bert Ambrose had upon his protégée. Everything she did had to be personally seen and specifically sanctioned by Bert Ambrose. She was not permitted to make any independent decisions.

When all this is said, it was the undoubted fact that the relationship seemed to suit Kathy Kirby. She was happy to be absolved from the responsibility of decision making. After honing her skills on the cabaret circuit she proved more than ready when the opportunity to record was presented to her.

The record for which she is best remembered was a re-make of a song called 'Secret Love.' This had been a huge hit for the remarkable Doris Day in the 1950s. Doris Day was a consummate singer and actress (as female actors were then called) and had twenty-five hits in the United States. She also had several British hits before the UK charts were introduced in 1952; she had many more afterwards. 'Secret Love' was her greatest success, reaching Number 1 in the charts on both sides of the Atlantic. The song spent twenty-nine weeks in the UK charts. Although this was fifty years ago from today, it was less than a decade from the time that Kathy Kirby recorded the same song.

The arrangement was a new one; the arranger was the brilliant Charles Blackwell who had an inspirational talent in matching the arrangement to the strongest attribute of the individual artist. He recognised that Kathy Kirby had a very good, very strong voice with an unusual ability to pitch and sustain a note in the upper vocal register. Charles Blackwell did not seek to replicate the Doris Day sound which had been perfect for the 1950s audience but might be perceived to be a little 'treacly' for the apparently more sophisticated 60s. In fact, it was not any attempt at sophistry that hit the mark, rather the adoption of an unique (though later much copied) sound which was based upon Bobby Graham's 'four to the bar' stamp or flam beat. This had already been used on a number of hit records and was used on many more afterwards. Although the strength of the sound is easily identifiable, it is not the most obvious sound to those who listen to the vocal and melody rather than the driving rhythm section. Kathy Kirby's became a big thumping beat version of the song with a very powerful vocal sound. The record was an immediate hit climbing to Number 4 in the charts and staying in the charts for eighteen weeks. It overlapped with her next hit 'Let Me Go Lover' which reached Number 10 in the charts in February 1964.

These, though, were not her first hits. Her first hit record had a vocal version of the Shadows instrumental hit 'Dance On' which had been the Shadows seventh hit and fourth Number 1 when it topped the charts in December of 1962. The Kathy Kirby rendition made Number 11 but most who remember the song do so without great affection or admiration.

After 'Let Me Go Lover' Kathy Kirby had a hit with her next release 'You're The One.' Bobby Graham and has good reason to remember recording this number, and so does Charles Blackwell: "Although it was a morning session at the Decca studios, for some reason Bobby arrived late. The fixer on the session was Charlie Katz who liked punctuality. By the time Bobby came into the building, about three quarters of an hour late, Bobby had fortified himself and was drunk. Whether he had been topping up from the night before, I wouldn't know. I saw him walking along the corridor downstairs; it was quite a wide corridor, about twelve feet wide. As he walked along Bobby was lurching from side to side banging first one wall then the other. Anyway, he made it into the studio, his kit was already set up and he could see in the studio it was just a few of the usual players. What he didn't know, and I didn't tell him, was that I had wired up to the adjoining studio and had a seventy piece orchestra set up there. Bobby put his cans on and I counted in. All of a sudden this huge orchestral sound played through the cans and Bobby had no idea what was going on. He looked around the studio with this startled expression on his face. He was looking round to see where I had hidden the orchestra. "After the session I remember Charlie Katz poking his head round the door and saying "Bobby I want a word with you." "

Bobby Graham always found Kathy Kirby a delight to work with "she was a very kind person and a very nice lady." She was even nice when Bobby was joined at a session by his wife June and his baby daughter Tracy. Kathy Kirby held the baby and didn't seem to mind when Tracy wet herself but mostly wet Kathy Kirby.

Then there was the fabulous Petula Clark. Pet Clark was a child prodigy who first came into the public eye as a six year old during the 1940s and sang in the Victory in Europe celebrations at the end of World War Two. She had, in fact, been entertaining the troops for some time, appearing in over two hundred shows for the forces.

She went on to achieve enduring success as a singer and actress. She had six chart hits between 1954 and 1959, her records spending a total of eighty weeks in the top twenty over this five year period.

If this was good then the 1960s were an even more fertile time for her recordings. Her first, and only, UK Number 1 hit entered the charts in January 1961. It was a song called 'Sailor' which had a haunting melody and especially suited Petula Clark's voice. The same year she married Claude Wolff and set up home with him in France. She had met her husband when he was instrumental in persuading her to record in French.

In 1962 she was visited in Paris by Tony Hatch

bringing with him his new song. Tony Hatch was a brilliant producer and arranger and part of a very productive songwriting team with his wife Jackie Trent. Jackie Trent was also a very accomplished singer; she reached Number 1 in the charts in 1965 with 'Where Are You Now.'

From the first time he worked with her, Bobby found Petula Clark a joy to work with: "she was always so happy and friendly." The first of her records upon which Bobby played was the Tony Hatch/Jackie Trent song: it was called 'Downtown'. Although there was a lot of brass on the recording it was made without a full blown orchestra. There has been a lot of contention as to who it was that played drums on this recording. Some believed it was Kenny Clare and there have also been claims by an American drummer. This latter claim may have some validity because Petula Clark did re-record the song in the States. However, the hit version has Bobby Graham on drums; Bobby has a clutch of contemporary music papers and magazines which confirm that he was the drummer. "It's not the clippings; I only have to listen to it and I know it's me."

After 'Downtown', which reached Number 2 in November 1964 and spent over three months in the charts, Bobby worked with Petula Clark many more times. "She was utterly professional at every session. She was always prepared to listen to others and while many others I worked with always knew best, she would value the opinion of anyone who had an opinion to express. The flexibility of her approach was a revelation. I liked her a lot. She was always smiling. She is a very warm, lovely lady."

Another female vocalist that Bobby found stimulating to work with was Brenda Lee – 'Little Miss Dynamite.' Bobby believes that he only played on one session with Brenda Lee, which is probably correct as she did almost all of her recording in her native America. However, the one session was memorable.

Brenda Lee was born Brenda Mae Tarpley on the 11th of December 1944 in Atlanta, Georgia. She made her first record when she was eleven years old, on the 21st of May 1956. She then shot to fame as a fifteen year old with 'Sweet Nothins' which was a big hit on both sides of the Atlantic. For the next five years she was a fixture in the charts in the UK and America with twenty-three chart hits in the UK, spending a colossal 210 weeks in the charts.

In 1962, during a Jackie Wilson concert at the Fairgrounds Coliseum in Nashville, Tennessee she met her future husband, Ronnie. They married on the 24th of April 1963, when Brenda was still seventeen years old, and they remain happily married still.

She toured the UK regularly; on one occasion her record company, Brunswick, which was part of the Decca group, suggested she should record in London, so a session was arranged and The Musical Stuntmen brought in to play on the recording. The producer was the South African born Mickie Most, one of the most influential producers and managers of the pop music era.

From the moment that Brenda Lee joined them in the studio Bobby says, "she was great fun, great to work with and with no big ego; we all warmed to her straight away. It is amazing how this helps in a session."

She was recording a Carter/Lewis song 'Is it True'. There was a technical glitch in the control box and so the recording was temporarily halted while a tape machine was replaced. The musicians began to jam, playing nothing in particular but such was their rapport that the sound quickly gelled. The other players, Big Jim Sullivan, Jimmy Page, Alan Weighell and Arthur Greenslade were regular musical companions of Bobby and they had an almost telepathic musical understanding.

Someone asked Miss Lee if she knew 'What'd I Say', a song which had been a top ten hit for Jerry Lee Lewis in

1961, although perhaps a song more associated with Ray Charles. She did and moments later her powerful voice was belting it out with enormous gusto. Unbeknown to the musicians the tape machine had been replaced and the song had been recorded. It was a 'one take' recording and became the B side of 'Is it True'; Bobby remains firmly of the view that it should have been released as the A side because the recording highlighted Brenda Lee's huge vocal power. In the event the record was a hit making it to Number 17 in the charts in November of 1964.

In fact, 'What'd I Say' was released as an A side on the continent where it did very well. Curiously, it seems not to have been released in America as a single.

The session also produced two more tracks although neither is as memorable as the impromptu recording they made that day.

John Carter, half of the song writing duo Carter/Lewis and another musical polymath also remembers the session: "I was singing backing vocals on some of the tracks. When this impromptu session started I was knocked out. It was a terrific team there that day. The power of Bobby's drumming, the strength of Big Jim and Jimmy's guitars, Alan Weighell's precision bass playing and Arthur Greenslade's haunting piano made for a great sound."

John Carter did a lot of recording with Bobby Graham. This session stood out. "It was a real example of a great singer fitting in with the musicians because of a natural musical empathy. We all enjoyed it."

Indeed, Bobby enjoyed recording with all of these singers and many other female vocalists too. Amongst others he recorded with were Shirley Bassey, Cilla Black, Lulu, Patsy Ann Noble and Twinkle.

"I enjoyed every session with them all. I have lots of happy memories."

The Kinks

Which group did Bobby Graham most enjoy playing with? Ask him that direct question and the answer is immediate: "It was The Kinks; they were just fantastic."

They are a fascinating group who, for four decades, have made an enormous contribution to our musical heritage. Their background and genesis is interesting. Ray and Dave Davies were the seventh and eighth of eight children, and the only sons of Frederick George Davies and his wife Annie Florence Davies. Ray was born in 1944 and Dave three years later. By the time the boys were born the family lived in a modest terraced house in Muswell Hill, North London.

It was a fairly musical household; the Davies' family bought an upright piano from Berry & Co on the Holloway Road, very close to where Joe Meek had his recording studio. The piano was installed in the front room of the Davies' household; the room also housed a radiogram. Ray and Dave's six sisters were keen on the music of the day so the boys grew up to the sounds of a diverse range of music – everything from Johnny Ray and Perry Como to Hank Williams. As the 1950s progressed the sounds included those of Bill Haley and The Comets, Elvis Presley and Little Richard. There was also Big Band Music from the likes of The Ted Heath Orchestra and skiffle from Lonnie Donegan. Another musical factor was the regular Saturday night family parties at their home where music was the constant theme.

By the time the boys began to buy their own records they tended to choose guitar based music from the leading players of the day – Les Paul, Chet Atkins and Duane Eddy provided early influences; they also liked guitar-playing singers such as Chuck Berry.

Despite the three-year age gap, the brothers were united by their joint enthusiasm for music. Although conventional sibling tensions arose then as they have done ever since, they played music together from a young age. They started with the piano and then graduated to guitars. For his thirteenth birthday Ray was given his first guitar by his mother and sister Rene. Tragically on that same day Rene died as the result of a heart attack; the consequence of childhood rheumatic fever which had left her with a damaged heart.

In spite of this tragedy Ray took to his guitar and became a prolific player in a relatively short time. Two years after his brother acquired his first guitar Dave got one of his own, a Harmony Meteor, bought on hire purchase by his father. The brothers practised and rehearsed together. From the outset their guitar styles were very different. Ray played in a more classical, acoustic manner whereas, even as a young teenager, Dave was playing with a much more raw style. He developed his own riffs and unique playing method and was basically self-taught. Both, but especially Ray, were helped by their brother-in-law Michael, who was married to their sister Peg. Michael was a talented musician and gave his time unstintingly. Ray enjoyed these guitar lessons and was introduced to a much wider musical spectrum.

Dave bought a second-hand amplifier with which he began to experiment. He developed some of the effects which were to form part of the unique sound of The Kinks only a couple of years later.

By the time that Ray was seventeen and Dave fourteen they were playing gigs together. They were soon joined by Pete Quaife who lived locally and was a good six string guitarist. The story goes that the three drew lots to see who would play bass guitar. Pete perceived himself to have lost; he became the bass guitarist and a very accomplished one.

They recruited a drummer named John Start who was lucky enough to own a complete drum kit; this was very unusual at the time. The group played as the Ray Davies Quartet and then RDQ with Ray and Dave alternating on vocals. Dave tried to encourage Ray to take the role of main vocalist. After forty years there is some confusion as to the chronology of events and particularly whether RDQ were playing together when Ray, being three years older than Dave, began to broaden his musical experience by playing with other bands. He auditioned for and then played with the Dave Hunt Band. Dave Hunt was a trombone player and occasional vocalist; the band that took his name played an eclectic mix of jazz and blues that bordered on rhythm and blues. Dave recollects that whilst watching his brother play a gig in central London he was impressed by another band playing the same gig. Although very raw, Dave liked their sound. They were called The Rolling Stones.

Ray was similarly impressed by this group. Some time later, when the drummer with Alexis Korner's band confided in Ray that he was thinking of leaving to take up an invitation to join The Rolling Stones, Ray encouraged him to do because he thought they had an exciting sound. Charlie Watts followed his advice.

Recollections diverge not just on chronology in the sense of what happened next but on nomenclature too. At about this time Ray formed another group called The Blues Messengers with Hamilton King, who was the vocalist with the Dave Hunt Band. Hamilton King was an accomplished harmonica player and singer. According to Dave's recollection, they were also joined by a blues enthusiast drummer named Mick Fleetwood; he later formed Fleetwood Mac. Much of the sound that the Blues Messengers made was obviously blues driven. It unquestionably had a great influence on the other group that Ray still played with which, by now had changed its name from RDQ to The Ramrods. By the middle of 1963 they had acquired a new drummer, Micky Willett who, although an excellent drummer, was several years older than the others. He was in his late twenties which to Ray and Dave must have seemed like he came from a different generation. It may have been the advice of Pete Quaife's girlfriend Nicola that led to Mickey Willett having such a short tenure with the group. Although she had no comment on his drumming abilities, she felt he did not fit their image; her view seems ultimately to have prevailed.

Before Mickey Willett left, he and Pete Quaife met two former public schoolboys, Grenville Collins and Robert Wace, who expressed an interest in joining them. They were looking to manage aspiring groups and Robert fancied himself as a vocalist. Things went well on the society circuit into which the group found themselves thrust. Robert Wace's singing career came to an abrupt end when he realised that the audience at an East End youth club were less receptive to his café style than had been his society friends.

Mickey Willett's replacement was Johnny Green whose image more closely fitted in with the others. By now the group enjoyed a considerable following in and around Muswell Hill. Their managers were keen that they should sign a proper contract. They formed a management company called Boscobel Productions and persuaded the group's members to sign it. As they were all under twenty-one (then the age of majority) their parents were obliged to sign too. Grenville Collins and Robert Wace had the charming but, frankly superior manner, which proved persuasive and the contract was duly signed. This was later to be the source of regret to the group's members.

Things moved apace. Shortly afterwards they played a gig which was attended by an agent named Arthur Howes. He saw around the rougher edges of their playing and liked their music. Arthur Howes had a major input into the nationwide tours that were so popular at the time. He met the managers and terms were agreed for him to act as their agent.

There was yet another change of drummer. Johnny Green left and so a replacement was needed. Auditions were held. One of those who attended was Mick Avory. Although not all aspects of his audition were happy, he was nonetheless invited to join the group.

There were also two further changes of name, firstly, in deference to Bo Diddley's song of the same name to The Boll Weevils and then to The Ravens. Both lacked the cachet of a top ten group.

A meeting with Larry Page proved to be the next major influence upon the group's progress. Larry Page had started his show business career as a singer in the late fifties and had moved into the broader musical world where he played a multi-faceted role. He had an almost unerring commercial instinct; this was prophetically accurate with the young foursome that he took to at once. He encouraged Ray Davies to write songs and suggested that the next 'musts' were to find a record producer and, when having done so, to get a recording contract.

Larry Page suggested they meet an American record producer named Shel Talmy. They all hit it off straight-away; Shel Talmy arranged a series of auditions. Decca Records were unimpressed, but then The Beatles had failed to impress them too. Shel Talmy and his charges had more success at Pye. So, after an historic meander through the early years of one of the most significant groups in the history of pop music we are ready for Bobby Graham to enter their lives.

By the time of their first proper recording session Ray Davies was a prolific writer. He had already written 'You Really Got Me.' The group's demo recording of this, and other of his songs had not found favour with Larry Page.

The first session was recorded at the Pye Studios at Marble Arch. The decision was taken at executive level by Shel Talmy, Arthur Howes and Larry Page that the group's first release should be a re-working of the Little Richard original 'Long Tall Sally.'

Mick Avory, although a member, was not yet established as a fixture in the group so it was decided to use a session drummer. Ray had heard Bobby playing on other records: "I was bowled over by his style and power which was very reminiscent of Dave Clark's drumming on all of his hits." (Ray Davies was very perceptive.) "Bobby Graham added a tidiness and a dimension to our sound."

The session went well. The group could scarcely believe the finished sound. Shel Talmy had worked magic in retaining the unique Dave Davies guitar sound. Bobby Graham's drumming was integral to the mix and Ray Davies' vocals sound fresh even after forty years.

There was a problem. The first single was recorded with a good B side 'I Took My Baby Home' but the group still did not have a distinctive name. The solution was found in a public house one evening when comment was made about the faux-leather capes and kinky boots being worn. Larry Page heard someone call them Kinks and took the unilateral decision that this should be the group's name. And so it was.

A television appearance on *Ready Steady Go* gave the single and the newly-named group much welcome publicity and all concerned were delighted that the record made the charts; albeit only to Number 42 and only for one week.

There followed a hectic and enjoyable touring schedule. There are some memorable parts of touring with The Dave Clark Five and The Hollies. Whilst touring their follow up single 'You Still Want Me' was released. This had been recorded at the first Pye session. It flopped. The tour continued but reaching the lower echelons of the charts with a first single and achieving nothing with the second did little for the group's confidence. Nonetheless, it was not long before they were back in the studio.

In contrast to the limited recollection of so many sessions by so many players, almost all present remember the next time The Kinks recorded. In fact, the next session proved not to be definitive. Shel Talmy insisted that, although Mick Avory was now a permanent member of the group, he should be replaced for the session by Bobby Graham, with Avory playing tambourine. They recorded 'You Really Got Me' but no-one was thrilled with the result. After much pleading by Ray Davies, Larry Page and Shel Talmy were persuaded to re-record the song. Such a course, especially for an unproven group, was extremely unusual.

Pye Records were unhappy with the proposal but a session was booked at the IBC Studios that were in a basement at Portland Place. Arthur Greenslade played piano, Ray Davies rhythm guitar, Pete Quaife bass guitar, Mick Avory on tambourine with Dave Davies on lead guitar. Bobby Graham was on drums.

Ray Davies recalls the session: " We did one take and I was grateful that they were letting us do that but I still wasn't completely happy. There was a lot of clock watching and even Bobby Graham, who was one of the most supportive session men, glanced at his watch when I asked Shel if we could do another take. He reluctantly agreed. When Dave played the opening chords Bobby Graham forgot the complicated introduction he had planned and just thumped one beat on the snare drum with as much power as he could muster. For the next three minutes he was one of us.

Then came Dave's solo. In the forty years that have passed there has been a great deal of speculation whether it was Dave who played the solo. The answer is categorically "yes." It was sensational. There was a thunderous silence in the studio after the track ended. The backing track was played and Arthur Greenslade listened with a much keener interest than was usual for these seasoned and sometimes jaundiced professionals. Then Bobby packed his drums, smiling at Ray Davies as he did so. The session men had done their bit so they left before the vocals were added.

The record was released in the summer of 1964 and was a sensation. By August it was Number 1 in the charts and launched The Kinks on a spectacular trajectory.

Bobby's recollection of this session is not exactly the same as the others. "I had got on really well with them when we had recorded 'Long Tall Sally' and some other tracks. They were almost unique in that they didn't see me as an interloper. They seemed to respect me as a session player. The second time we recorded 'You Really Got Me' was better but not quite right. Ray had wanted me to play some pretty complicated bits which I didn't feel fitted in; I thought it needed a much more basic drum pattern. After running through it a couple of times I decided to go off script and do something different. Dave played the intro and I dived in with a snare shot. It worked. Then there was Dave's amazing lead break. We were all very happy with it. I played on lots of other sessions with The Kinks. There was some talk about me joining The Kinks but I turned it down because I'd had enough of touring and was a successful session man."

The recording of the next Kinks single occurred during the currency of a tour. Many of the dates on the tour were in the north of England. A session was arranged which involved the group travelling down to London late one night. This was in the knowledge that they would have to leave to travel back early the following afternoon. Three hours was allowed for the session. It was important that the backing track should be laid down quickly.

Once again session players were used. Some think that Perry Ford played piano although Bobby does not recall this himself. Bobby Graham played drums. Ray Davies' recollection is that Bobby was displeased at the specific suggestion that he should play a particular infill between the second and third verses. "I don't think Bobby was very happy. It was a simple request but I thought he got annoyed. Anyway, he played it with such splendid venom that it took on an entirely new sound, a sound of its own." Again, Bobby has a slightly different recall. The infill was a copy of that played on 'It's So Easy' the Buddy Holly song.

The track 'All Day And All of the Night' was released quickly. Chart success meant that a follow up was normally released in the weeks that its predecessor was beginning to slide down the charts. 'You Really Got Me' spent twelve weeks in the charts and overlapped with its successor .

'All Day And All Of The Night' would surely have reached Number 1 but for the fact that The Beatles released 'I Feel Fine' a few weeks later. This kept The Kinks off the top spot; they settled for Number 2 although their next single 'Tired of Waiting For You' reached Number 1.

In between these two singles The Kinks found time to record an album *The Kinks*. In 1964 the target market was for singles some of which literally sold millions. The LP was an integral part of the process of retaining public interest in chart scoring groups. Then, as now, singles were often taken from albums. However, it was not commonly the case that a great deal of studio time was devoted to creating albums.

The use of session musicians was the more important to complete a project in days rather than weeks. Bobby Graham played on The Kinks first album, an experience he thoroughly enjoyed. He played on every track but one, 'Sobbing' and Perry Ford played piano on all piano tracks. Jimmy Page played twelve string guitar on 'Bald Headed Woman' which had been composed by Shel Talmy.

"What I really like about The Kinks is that they were the first group to be completely up front and acknowledge the contribution session players made. More than that, they were a great band. Ray Davies is a musical genius and Dave Davies is a spectacular guitarist. I really enjoyed working with them. I was delighted when Ray asked me to play on his 1998 re-recording of 'You Really Got Me.'"

What do others say of Bobby Graham's contribution to The Kinks' records. It could not be put better than by Shel Talmy himself: "I am on record as saying that Bobby Graham is the best UK session drummer ever. Could I add to that? His feel for the music was almost telepathic. You only had to ask him once and he did. His timing was sensational. He is a great player."

Dave Davies is similarly complimentary. "When The Kinks started recording with Bobby Graham I realised what great rock drumming was all about. He was one of a small band of English musicians who had the right attitude. Bobby would hit the drums so hard the engineers never had any trouble recording him. He was a great inspirational drummer."

They were very happy days.

Dave Berry

Dave Berry was brought up with music. His father was a talented jazz drummer playing in and around Sheffield where Dave was born and raised. He was exposed to music from a young age. His early musical influences, his father apart, were mostly American; he loved the music of Gene Vincent and, in particular, Chuck Berry. In 1960 he formed his own group, Dave Berry and the Cruisers. They were heavily influenced by rhythm and blues and swiftly gained a large following in and around Sheffield. Their reputation spread and it was not long before Dave signed a recording contract with Decca Records.

His recording career began in 1963. From the start, session musicians played on his recordings; from then on he had a road band but when recording session players were used. Bobby Graham played on almost all, if not all of the sessions over the next years.

Dave Berry explains: "I had recorded a couple of demos in 1962 that were backed by most of the musicians from Joe Brown's Bruvvers. It was great playing with a name band. Neither of the demos was released. Mickie Most and Mike Smith were in charge of the recording."

In 1963 Dave Berry recorded a Chuck Berry number 'Memphis Tennessee' which crept into the top twenty in September of that year but then stayed in the charts almost until Christmas. His follow up singles 'My Baby Left Me' with explosive guitar playing by Jimmy Page, and a cover version of 'Baby It's You' also made the lower reaches of the charts in January and April of 1964. However, it was his next record for which he will always be remembered.

By the time that Dave Berry recorded the Geoff

Stephens composition 'The Crying Game' Mickie Most was no longer on the scene and Mike Smith, was in charge of the recording. (This was not the same Mike Smith who played in The Dave Clark Five.)

Dave Berry can remember the line-up: "John Paul Jones on bass, Bobby Graham on drums, I think it was Reg (Earl) Guest on keyboards and Jimmy Page on guitar and it was definitely Big Jim Sullivan on lead guitar. Stan Barrett played the tuned drums."

The recording is memorable for several reasons, the most significant of which is that Big Jim Sullivan arrived at the Decca studio with a new toy. It was a De Armand wah-wah pedal which had the effect of distorting the guitar sound. Big Jim was already renowned for his incredible facility of sound distortion by the simple expedient of bending and pulling the guitar strings on the fretboard. He was also among the first, in fact probably the first, to use a fuzzbox which he had used to great effect on PJ Proby's 'Hold Me.'

But the wah-wah pedal added a new dimension to his virtuoso skills. It had not been planned that he should use it on the recording of 'The Crying Game' but on hearing what it could do, Mike Smith readily agreed to its use. The sound was amazing.

"I was absolutely stunned by the sound it made," says Dave Berry. "I think we all were. It turned out much better than I had ever expected."

Bobby Graham was equally captivated. "I never ceased to be amazed by Jim's playing but this was special."

Big Jim Sullivan is characteristically modest about this defining sound in sixties music: "I was always on the lookout for new sounds and the wah-wah pedal was completely different to anything else I had used before. It worked well and made an interesting noise. I think the song really suited Dave's voice but it is nice that it all gelled together."

The record reached Number 5 in the charts in August

of 1964, and remained in the charts for twelve weeks. It has ever since been the song associated with Dave Berry but by no means marked the end of his chart success. His next but one release 'Little Things' enjoyed identical success to 'The Crying Game,' Number 5 and twelve weeks in the charts. Another record 'This Strange Effect,' for which he is also known, had lesser success in the UK but enjoyed spectacular results in Holland. Some years later Bobby recorded a version of the same song specifically for the Dutch market this time as Dave Berry's producer. An interesting version of the same song features on Bobby's new CD.

Dave Berry was impressed by Bobby's drumming: "He was an excellent player. I mean no disrespect to others but he was more suited to the stuff I was recording than some of the drummers whose hearts were still in jazz. He could do the triple paradiddles if you wanted them but he wouldn't play them just because he could."

Stan Barrett also remembers the Dave Berry recordings and Bobby Graham's playing. "When Bobby arrived on the scene he was immediately flavour of the month but not just for that month but for many months to come. I remember him arriving at Decca and immediately realising that he was not a shy person. I later realised he was lacking in self-confidence although he was a brilliant drummer. He had this fantastic approach to drumming; it was the sort of music that would sell records. He became the number one session drummer although he had his problems. He was not the best sight reader. I used to try to help so when the morning tea break came I would say "would you like me to talk you through the next part of the session?" But Bobby would be off down the pub with me clinging to his jacket trying to hold him back."

Them

Even though Bobby played on hundreds of sessions, it might nonetheless be expected that he would have an instant recall of the sessions on which he helped to produce some memorable music.

"No, it was not like that. Often, we would spend about forty minutes on a track, possibly running through it only once or twice before the actual recording. It was the norm to record four tracks in a three hour session and an ordinary working day would involve three separate sessions. The recording was not necessarily the finished product; In fact it rarely was. The producer and engineer would see to that after we had left. Although multi track machines were much less sophisticated in those days, post recording mixing could produce a more refined article."

So it is that people remind Bobby of sessions he played on about which he has no recall. In contrast, a session that Bobby will never forget took place at the Decca 2 Studio on the 5th of July 1964. The session was to record a number of tracks with Them.

Them was a five piece group from Belfast who were making their playing and recording debut on the mainland. Their singer was Van Morrison who was then a month short of his nineteenth birthday. 'Van the Man' has a richly deserved reputation as a curmudgeonly older man. In 1964 he was a curmudgeonly young man, looking as he did, like a dissolute, young Dylan Thomas.

Records show that the group made their live debut in London on the evening of the 4th of July although this may be a day out. They were the supporting act to Sounds Incorporated an instrumental group who had made the lower reaches of the charts in April 1964 with 'The Spartans' and who were about to enjoy slightly lesser success with their only other chart entry 'Spanish Harlem' which reached the charts that July.

At the gig Them were awful. They played two sets the second of which was marginally better than the first. Van Morrison was apparently fortified with copious quantities of Irish whiskey between sets and this seems to have calmed his nerves.

The recording session was under the musical direction of Arthur Greenslade who was already very well-regarded both as a session piano/keyboard player and also as a musical director. He found Them to be an interesting group but "pretty raw."

At the recording session Arthur Greenslade and American producer Bert Berns told the group that Bobby Graham was to play drums. The band was furious and threatened to walk out. Van Morrison was vocal in his disagreement with the use of a session player but ultimately his trenchantly expressed attitude was to no avail. There are, at least, two stories of what happened. The romantic version is that Jimmy Millings, Them's drummer, played in one booth and Bobby Graham in another, with only Bobby's kit being wired up to record. The truth is less subtle; no such attempt was made to assuage his, or the group's feelings, and Jimmy Millings simply went back to his digs. Bobby, alone played on the sessions that were recorded that day.

At least four tracks were recorded at this session 'Baby Please Don't Go,' 'Gloria', 'Here Comes the Night' and 'All For Myself.' They were all very good. Decca released 'Baby Please Don't Go' on the A side of the group's first single with 'Gloria' as the B side. The record entered the charts in January of 1965 and reached Number 10 the next month. The follow up single, 'Here Comes the Night', was released as soon as its predecessor started to slip down the charts. Interestingly, it is the B side of the first hit that many people associate with the 'Them' sound; it has had an enduring popularity.

"The session was unusual in a number of ways. My recollection is that I was not originally booked to play on the session but after they had run through the numbers at the studio I was called in. I was used to playing with groups who didn't exactly welcome me with open arms but the lack of reception, especially from Van Morrison was obvious. As soon as we started things changed and we got on OK. Well, at least, I think we must have done because I was invited to play on another session with Them which we all enjoyed. In fairness to Van, he had a fantastically powerful voice for an eighteen year old. I think he realised that Arthur Greenslade was just doing his job and wanted to get the best sound."

Them had their biggest hit with 'Here Comes the Night' which entered the charts in March of 1965 and made it to Number 2, remaining in the charts for almost three months. But that was then end of their chart success although, of course, Van Morrison has enjoyed an illustrious stage and recording career ever since.

Big Jim Sullivan, who continues to play and remains an immensely talented musician, has recent experience of Van Morrison. In order to understand the perspective of Big Jim's views it is worth recalling that he has been at the top of his profession for over forty years. He joined Marty Wilde's Wildcats in the 1950s and backed Eddie Cochran on his 1960 tour of the UK. Over the next decade he, like Bobby Graham, played on thousands of tracks, hundreds of which made the charts. He has, literally, seen them all. "Just recently I played with Van Morrison and I came to realise that money can't make a decent human being out of you. He is as unhappy a person as I have ever seen. My stay with Van was very short lived and the lesson learned from him will stay with me for a long time."

Other Favourites

When Bobby Graham first recorded with Billy Fury, he and Billy were already firm friends, having toured together and got on very well. Billy Fury had had great success since he first made the charts in 1959 and had three consecutive top five singles in the second half of 1961.

Ronald Wycherley was born in Liverpool in April 1941 (although some record his birth a year earlier) and had approached Larry Parnes with some material he had written for himself. After a brief audition he was signed to the Parnes stable and swiftly renamed Billy Fury. His versatility made him a very attractive proposition for Parnes who, although initially inclined to cast him as a rock 'n'roller soon realised his great facility for singing ballads. Parnes also recognised the fact that his introverted newcomer responded best when he had good musical backing. Parnes arranged backing by The Blue Flames with pianist Clive Powell, later to become Georgie Fame, drummer Red Reece, guitarist Colin Green (currently Shirley Bassey's musical director), and bassist Tex Makins.

Bobby Graham recorded with Billy Fury on a number of sessions from about Christmas 1962. "In a sense it was a little unusual. I hadn't played on his earlier recordings but somehow I felt a lot closer to him musically than a lot of other artists. I enjoyed playing with Billy. He had a very controlled voice and knew how to exploit his range to maximum effect."

Bobby played on five hits for Billy Fury the first of which was 'Like I've Never Been Gone' which reached Number 3 in the charts in the spring of 1963. Bobby especially enjoyed recording 'It's Only Make Believe' which had been a Number 1 hit for Conway Twitty in 1958.

"It showed what he could do. It is a very subtle interpretation of a very good song. Lots of people have recorded it but Billy's version is amongst the best."

Bobby also played on Billy Fury's last Decca hit 'Give Me Your Word' which made it only to the lower reaches of the top thirty and signalled the end of Billy Fury's real chart success. During his time with Decca he had made the charts with all but three of his releases.

He enjoyed a minor revival in 1982 when two Polydor recordings made it to Numbers 57 and 58 respectively. Sadly his last chart entry was a posthumous one. He died in January 1983, his life having been plagued with ill health following childhood illness. Bobby expresses the views of many when he says: "I was very sad and sorry to hear that Billy had gone. Nice man. Very nice man. I went to his funeral and the church choir sang a special Ivor Raymonde version of 'Like I've Never Been Gone' and it was a really sad moment."

Somewhat surprisingly, a group that Bobby always enjoyed playing with were The Bachelors. They now describe themselves as 'The Original Irish Boy Band' although much of their appeal was to the parents' generation. They were clean cut, charming and the antithesis of the emergent anti-authoritarian groups. They were from Dublin and comprised two brothers, Dec and Con Cluskey and their (then) friend John Stokes. The Cluskey brothers sang and played guitar and John Stokes played the double bass. Their sound involved close harmony and was unique.

Dec was the organiser, Con had the great voice and John appeared to be the quiet one. He was, though, many people's favourite. The Bachelors were very successful and sold millions of records. Their hits included 'I Believe', a remake of the Frankie Laine hit, 'Ramona' and 'I Wouldn't Change You For The World.'

"They were a very nice bunch of guys, easy to work

with and well rehearsed before each session." Bobby played on most of their hits and is slightly disappointed that his name does not appear on their otherwise informative website.

Tom Jones was another favourite. He had been singing in the clubs and pubs of South Wales since a young teenager. He sang with his backing group as Tommy Scott and The Senators. He had a very powerful voice and a huge personality.

By the time that Bobby met him he was managed by Gordon Mills and had changed his name to Tom Jones with his backing group becoming The Squires. Although Gordon Mills has been credited with discovering Tom Jones the real credit for that should, perhaps, go to Peter Sullivan who was a staff producer at Decca and who recognised the talent of the young Welshman.

Tom Jones first hit was 'It's Not Unusual' which stormed to Number 1 in the charts in 1965 and which is generally credited with being the shortest Number 1 of all time at one minute and fifty seven seconds. It was composed by Les Reed (who also composed 'Delilah' for Tom Jones) and produced by Peter Sullivan with the composer as musical director. The drummer for the session was Ronnie Verrall and a number of other members of The Ted Heath Orchestra also played on the track.

"I recall very clearly the first Tom Jones recording that we made at Decca No 2 studio," says Graham. "His producer was called Peter Sullivan. As I understood it Tom had been discovered by Gordon Mills. Gordon had been in the music industry for many, many years and had been a part of a group called The Viscounts. He had done very well for himself when he discovered Tom in Wales and brought him down to London. Tom always gyrates when he's singing, even in the studio, in the vocal booth. For us guys it looked really quite funny. I remember saying to Gordon Mills "Gordon you're wasting your money on this one son, he's never going to do anything!" Wrong again."

"The first session we did with him was 'Chills and Fever'. We also did another title on that session. Now over the years confusion has reigned as to who played drums on 'It's Not Unusual'. I had always got it locked in my brain that it was me. I spoke to Les Reed who was the arranger/composer of the song and he said it was Ronnie Verrall. What had happened was that we had actually recorded the song with Tom at the 'Chills and Fever' session but it was a version that didn't get released. They re-recorded a new version which was released seven or eight months later. Not so long ago, somebody sent me the original version that we did not use on a cassette."

Bobby played on number of Tom Jones' later hits including 'The Green Green Grass of Home.' "I remember that session well. Although everybody agrees it is a fantastic song and really suited Tom's voice, it sounded a bit strange in the studio. Then I heard it on the radio and could hardly believe it was what we had recorded."

Bobby found Tom Jones to be a delight to work with, casual, relaxed but very good at what he did. In the moments before recording started he would often tap Bobby Graham on the shoulder and utter his traditional greeting "Alright butt." The power of his voice was phenomenal; the original rawness held its thrall and retained its magic when he changed his habits from cigarettes and beer to champagne and cigars.

Another male superstar of the 1960s was Englebert Humperdinck. He had been a journeyman singer as Gerry Dorsey (his birth name was Arnold Gerald Dorsey). He was struggling as a touring singer when he, too, was approached by Gordon Mills who was already enjoying spectacular success with Tom Jones. Gordon Mills decided that a change of image was needed. It was thought that a change of name may provide a passport to success. They decided to adopt the name of the 19th century German composer, most famous for his fairy tale opera *Hansel und Gretel*; why such a choice was made remains unclear. So Gerry Dorsey became Englebert Humperdinck. He released three singles which did nothing in the UK but then had a spectacular year in 1967.

Bobby has only a vague recollection of the first session he played on with Englebert Humperdinck although the principal product of the session has been memorable. 'Release Me', produced by Peter Sullivan and arranged by Charles Blackwell was a massive hit in 1967 and set the singer on the road to stardom. Bobby played on a number of other sessions including the recording of another Les Reed number 'The Last Waltz' with the same producer but arranged by Les Reed. Such was Englebert's success that he was the biggest selling artist in the UK in 1967 and achieved the rare distinction of holding the top spot against competition from The Beatles.

"To be honest the sessions with Englebert were pretty bland from my perspective. Don't get me wrong it was obvious that he was going to do very well but my part was relatively nondescript."

Eden Kane was someone that Bobby had met and got on very well with during their time together on the Larry Parnes tours when Bobby was playing with Joe Brown and The Bruvvers. His first hit 'Well I Ask You' had reached Number 1 in 1961. Eden Kane was born Richard Sarstedt in India on the 29th of March 1942, his family returning to the UK when he was young. He formed a skiffle group with his younger brothers Peter and Robin. His siblings both enjoyed chart success in their own right and in their own names. Peter Sarstedt's first hit was with 'Where Do You Go To My Lovely' which went to Number 1 in 1969 and Robin who reached Number 3 with 'My Resistance is Low' seven years later.

Richard Sarstedt's first recording was an advertising jingle for Cadbury's Drinking Chocolate 'Hot Chocolate Crazy' which was a regular feature on Radio Luxemburg. He adopted the name Eden Kane, probably inspired by the film *Citizen Kane* and no doubt partly influenced by the same biblical connotations as with Adam Faith, who had changed his name from Terence Nelhams.

Eden Kane was a fashionably good-looking young man and his looks brought him a part in the 1960 film *Drinks All Round*. He had great success with four top ten hits from June 1961 to May of the following year. He made the charts for a fifth and final time in the early part of 1964 with 'Boys Cry' a track on which Bobby Graham played.

Bobby got on very well with Eden Kane and was pleased to renew his acquaintanceship in the studio. It was a song which particularly suited Eden Kane's vocal style. "He was a real gentleman who had a great sense of timing so he was very easy to play for. I was surprised he didn't have greater success but, then again, it was the time of the groups and the solo artists lost out a bit."

Another entirely different artist that Bobby remembers recording with was Benny Hill who, although best remembered as a comedian, had a lot of hit records too. Alfred Hawthorne Hill was born in Southampton in January 1924 and began his entertainment career in the forces playing in the revue *Stars in Battledress*. After he was demobbed he became a member of the club circuit adopting the name 'Benny' in homage to the great American comedian Jack Benny. His success was via radio then television; his style was always of the saucy postcard variety which was loved and reviled in almost equal measure.

When he started recording he maintained the same style and avoided censure or censor for his lyrics even though a more attentive broadcasting organisation should have seen through the vulgarity of songs such as 'Pepys' Diary' and 'Gather in the Mushrooms.' But Benny Hill was the master of the double entendre.

Bobby remembers, just, playing on the recording of 'Harvest of Love' which hit the charts in May of 1963. "He was like a lot of comedians I've met, he did not spend his time laughing and joking, quite the opposite; he was really quite serious but it all changed when he went into character when he could be very, very funny indeed."

A group that Bobby met and played with in the mid sixties was A Band of Angels. The group was formed by members of Harrow School. Mike D'Abo was a vocalist with the group. He remembers their first recording session on which Bobby played: "Lets face it, what sort of a reception would you expect for a bunch of public school boys who thought they were the next best thing. For the first time in my life I thought I had come from the wrong side of the tracks and not everyone made us welcome. Overall though we were looked after reasonably well. Bobby Graham in particular, went out of his way to make us feel welcome. Anyone warm and open got my vote. At the first session, after we had played, it was decided that I would be allowed to play piano on the recordings but no other member of the group was allowed to play their instrument. On what became the A side of our first single 'Me' I was singing the harmony but when they played back the recording the harmony was much more prominent than the melody. Bobby was a great drummer. He was so tight, sometimes in more ways than one, but he could produce this 'fat' sound which I think was unique. It had a steady pulse that got lots of radio play."

A Band of Angels were always on the cusp of success. Mike D'Abo was in fine voice when A Band of Angels recorded and released a song called 'Invitation.' It led to his being enticed from the group in 1966 to replace Paul Jones with Manfred Mann. He played with them on all of their later hits and still tours with The Manfreds as well as with his own band Mike D'Abo and the Mighty Quintet. He is also a successful writer; three of his most well known contributions to our musical heritage include the 'Finger of Fudge' Cadburys commercial as well as

'Build Me Up Buttercup' a Number 2 hit for The Foundations and 'Handbags and Gladrags' for Chris Farlowe.

"Yes I remember A Band of Angels coming to the studio. They were a nice bunch, I really liked them. It was pretty obvious that Mike was the driving force and was going places. I am not surprised he had done so well. He makes a great spaghetti bolognese too."

And what of the others?

"There were so many. Even when I look at the charts for the period I find it difficult to remember the sequence in which they were recorded. I enjoyed recording with Brian Poole, he was a very polished guy. I played on a couple of tracks with Hermans Hermits that I enjoyed and I remember doing a session with Rod Stewart. But don't ask me to remember them all."

A Spectoral Experience

Although many of the sessions on which Bobby Graham played had an air of mystery one stands out in his recollection as being "bizarre."

A session was booked at the old Olympic Sound Studios in Carlton Street, London without even the usual clue as to what sort of session it was to be. A number of the musicians asked but each was told the same thing, which was – nothing, though they were told it in slightly different ways. The upshot was that it was a secret.

As the result the players arrived at the studio with mixed emotions; there was a tingling of trepidation mingled with a hint of unease and a frisson of excitement.

The identity of the recording artist was soon revealed; it was Adrienne Posta a stunning young actress who was making her mark in the London of the sixties. She went on to make a huge number of films and television appearances.

Bobby was delighted to be working with her even though he was not aware that she was a singer. He was perplexed as to why there should be this shroud of mystery around the whole thing. The answer came soon enough when word went around the studio that the session was being produced by Andrew Loog Oldham and Phil Spector. The arranger was the redoubtable Charles Blackwell for whom Bobby always had the highest regard; he was, though, the soul of discretion and was obviously anxious not to breach any confidences.

Andrew Loog Oldham had shot to fame as the very young manager of the emergent Rolling Stones and who had gone on to propel them into the stratosphere. He was a consummate dealmaker who had, from nothing, insinuated his way into the highest echelons of pop music on both sides of the Atlantic. He had gone on to produce some of the Stones seminal work and will ever be regarded as their Svengali. He and the Stones had parted acrimoniously. He tells the full story in his excellent *Stoned* and *Stoned 2*.

Ironically, it was his gift for attracting publicity which had allowed him to achieve the trajectory that he had. Yet at this session it seemed that publicity was not on the agenda.

The clue to this may lie in the presence of his co-producer, Phil Spector. To his adherents, Phil Spector is the single most influential producer in the history of rock music. To more objective observers this assertion may include an element of hyperbole. What is beyond doubt is that he had enjoyed spectacular success, initially as a writer, producer and performer with The Teddy Bears and thereafter predominantly as a producer. The catalogue of artists he recorded is impressive. His use of session musicians is legendary. The world's most famous session players The Wrecking Crew are renowned not simply for their association with Phil Spector but also as a musical entity in their own right.

Phil Spector was known also to be a complex character given to occasional bouts of bizarre and irrational behaviour. It remains a matter of conjecture, why the creator of 'the Wall of Sound' did not wish to be identified as producing on this otherwise low key session.

Bobby saw Andrew Loog Oldham during the session. He was as manic as ever, darting hither and thither, full of ideas, some rather better than others. Although the word was abroad that it was Phil Spector co-producing he did not introduce himself or make his presence obvious during the session. Bobby is fairly sure that he spotted him in the control box of the studio.

"I looked up and saw this figure wearing a cloak; that was Phil Spector's sartorial hallmark of the time and I was pretty sure it was him. Any doubts I had were removed when the session got under way."

Although Phil Spector purported to ignore the musicians his musical influence soon became apparent. There were two pianists playing one piano; this was very 'Phil Spector.' Confirmation was made with the drums; these were played with a thunderous echo. Directions came on the PA from the control box and it was clear to hear that an American voice was controlling things in the background.

The product of the session was a record called 'Shang A Doo Lang' with a track called 'When A Girl Really Loves You' on the B side. (Which contextually sounds like a Benny Hill joke.) It did nothing to establish a singing career for the young actress although the overall sound was deemed to be "pretty good."

Bobby and The Wrecking Crew's drummer Hal Blaine have long been friends at a great geographical distance. They are mutual admirers. Bobby would quite like to have had the acknowledgement of playing with Phil Spector but it was not to be.

"It was a very interesting experience but weird, really weird."

The Pretty Things

As the early sixties passed so Bobby Graham evolved from being 'just' a session player to become a producer, too. Initially, it was not as the result of any great deliberation on Bobby's part; he did, though, spend a lot of time in the studio control box, talking with the sound engineers. Gradually, as though by some process of osmosis, he assimilated a good deal of knowledge about the production process. He also learned some of the subtleties used by the producer to turn a raw recording into the polished product ready for release.

One of the problems for the session drummer is the physical need to transport bulky kit to every session. After a few years, the buzz of playing at sessions waned with the reality that, even an ordinary day, might include nine kit movements over a triangle of studios. So a move into production would have dual benefits for Bobby Graham: less kit handling and the dynamism of helping to create the finished article.

A defining moment in Bobby's progression from player to producer arose directly from the studio behaviour, or more accurately, of the misbehaviour of the ironically named Pretty Things.

Historic recollection of the groups of the early 1960s generally awards the 'parental disapproval' mantle to The Rolling Stones. Certainly, the Stones attracted massive disapprobation from an older generation; their long hair, scruffy appearance, and disrespectful attitude were a byword for the liberalised vogue which was such anathema to the 'War' generation.

If the Stones were scruffy and long haired they were as nothing compared to The Pretty Things. The group was formed at Sidcup Art College where vocalist Phil May met guitarist Dick Taylor. They were joined by bass player John Stax, rhythm guitarist Brian Pendleton and, a little later but, highly significantly, by drummer Viv Prince. They were all still in their late teens and had adopted an anarchic attitude to authority and the older generation.

Phil May has described the cathartic moment when Viv Prince joined: "We were sort of novice lunatics. But then suddenly they hand us, like, the High Priest of Lunacy. And we all caught on very quickly."

Although Keith Moon is regarded as being the most obvious candidate for 'lunatic drummer' of the sixties, many recollect Keith Moon standing transfixed by Viv Prince's outrageous stage conduct with The Pretty Things. It is reasonable to infer that Keith Moon was, to an extent at least, influenced by Viv Prince. Phil May was said to have the longest hair of any rock artist of the time.

By the time 'the Pretties' began recording, this line-up was complete. They were signed to Fontana and had early success. Between June 1964 and February 1965 their first three releases 'Rosalyn', 'Don't Bring Me Down' and 'Honey I Need' charted at 41, 10 and 13 respectively. The time then came for them to make an album. Three major problems supervened. Firstly, the allotted studio time was just two days. There was nothing unusual about such a short time being allocated. It was often the case that a first album would largely, and often exclusively, comprise the recording of the group's stage set; a set with which they should be familiar. The limited time slot apparently grated with the group.

The second problem was that the producer, Jack Baverstock, found the group impossible to work with. Jack Baverstock was a highly experienced and very talented producer. His background, though, was of a different era and different genre. He had been producing middle of the road albums and some jazz for many years.

He was, by this time, in his late fifties and so of a different generation; one which attracted the opprobrium, rather than the respect, of the group.

The third and most significant difficulty arose from the behaviour of the group; it is summed up best by Bobby Graham's recollection of meeting Jack Baverstock in the corridor at Stanhope House, the home of both Fontana Records and Phillips Records in London.

"He was rushing down the corridor, red in the face and muttering to himself "the bastards, those little bastards, I hate those little bastards, they're animals, bloody animals, I hate them."

He had rushed from the studio where The Pretty Things were giving him an especially hard time. Bobby has some recollection that Jack Baverstock suffered with ulcers and the stress the young group had put him under had caused an eruption of the symptoms.

Jack Baverstock was in need of salvation and seeing Bobby Graham he found it. He asked Bobby if he fancied doing some producing. Although thrilled at the prospect Bobby tried to play it cool. "I wouldn't mind" he replied. This was good enough and it allowed Jack Baverstock to unburden himself of the responsibility of producing the new album.

It would be nice to record that Bobby found the experience of producing The Pretty Things first album one of unalloyed pleasure but to do so would be to rewrite history. After half an hour Bobby found it difficult to demur from Jack Baverstock's description of the group. However, things changed.

The Pretty Things were fundamentally a rhythm and blues group drawing much of their inspiration from the Chicago electric blues music that had also inspired the Stones. However, they had a different perspective on some of those whose music influenced them. Although they shared the Stones' following of Bo Diddley and Chuck Berry, they also developed their music by

acknowledging the brilliance of Jimmy Reed, Howlin'
Wolf and Muddy Waters. The derivation of the music
they played was obvious, but their take on the music was
their own. They played at a frenetic pace and could
change a song that may have been written as a folk tune
into a fast and furious R&B number.

Bobby Graham found the studio to be chaotic when
he arrived there. The group were wholly undisciplined
and consequently it very difficult to channel their energy
and their talent. Two things made the difference; Bobby
really liked their music and he admired the fact that they
were all very good players. Ironically, Bobby was
impressed to discover that they did not need to resort to
session players to augment their sound; except, that is, for
Viv Prince. This was not because he could not play but
because he was plastered.

"Don't get me wrong, Viv was a very good player. If
he was sober, no problem. Trouble was he was out of it.
Fortunately it was the drummer who was drunk so I was
able to step in and help."

It did not take very long for Bobby Graham to establish a rapport with the Pretties; although he finds it
difficult to allocate specific recollections to specific sessions, he has an abiding recollection of the sessions
generally. It was hopeless to book them for a 10am
session. This was tried but it led to frustrating waits for
Bobby, the sound engineers and all others participating in
the session. The group would wander in whenever it
suited them, normally at about 2pm, and always suffering
the consequences of having spent the previous night and
much of the morning partying. Little would be achieved
until early evening by which time they had started drinking again.

Viv Prince was often hopelessly drunk when he
arrived at the studio. Bobby remembers more than one
occasion when Viv sat at the kit seemingly ready to play
and then simply keeled over. Bobby resorted to the

simple expedient of dragging him to the corner of the studio and allowing him to sleep it off while Bobby took the drum chair.

In spite of these difficulties the sessions were ultimately very productive and some excellent tracks were recorded. The first album has easily stood the critical test of time and remains well regarded by purists as well as dedicated followers of the genre.

Dick Taylor, The Pretty Things lead guitarist, has fond memories of the sessions with Bobby Graham: "From our point of view it was great, it meant we had two drummers. Viv was an excellent drummer but he did drink a lot and sometimes couldn't play at the sessions. Even when he could, he and Bobby sometimes used to alternate on different takes of the same track. Right from the start we all felt that Bobby understood us but, of course, we didn't tell him. We really enjoyed recording with Bobby."

It also gave Bobby Graham the opportunity to have some of his own music recorded. Three of the tracks on The Pretty Things second album *Get The Picture* were written by Bobby: 'Can't Stand The Pain' 'Nine To Six Man' and 'You Don't Believe Me.' He also wrote the B sides of one of their singles.

Working with The Pretty Things was a baptism of fire for Bobby Graham. But it led to a very successful professional relationship and one which equipped Bobby very well for his career as a producer.

A French Adventure

As the sixties progressed and the complexion of popular music changed forever, Bobby Graham's enthusiasm for playing on sessions diminished. What had been great fun and had hardly seemed like work was now becoming tedious. The physical effort demanded had worn Bobby out. Having played on so many hit records the thought was beginning to impinge on his consciousness that he did not have much tangible proof of the success that he had undoubtedly achieved. He needed a fresh challenge.

By now Bobby had had more than a taste of producing. He looked to the future and saw the challenge he would relish; he decided he would like to produce as well as to play. In producing records he perceived a dimension of control that had been lacking in the session playing.

Bobby began to work for a French record company called Disc Barclay that was owned by a multi millionaire named Eddie Barclay. Eddie was a colourful man who knew what he wanted and how to get it; he did not always take the most traditional route to success. Eddie Barclay sent a number of French Artists to London in the hope of emulating the 'English Sound.'

In 1967 the Eddie Barclay label asked Bobby to produce an album for the French market. It was credited to 'Le(s) London All Stars,' a delightful Franglais phrase and was entitled *British Percussion*. Bobby assembled a very impressive line-up of musicians with John McLoughlin on guitar, Alan Weighell on bass and both Andy White and Ronnie Verrall on drums. A major contribution was made by Jimmy Page; he played lead guitar on every track and co-wrote three of the tracks with Bobby Graham. The production of the album was revolutionary using ping pong stereo percussion effects and creating a very distinctive sound.

One of the French artists Eddie Barclay sent to the UK to record was a rock'n'roll singer named Eddy Mitchell; he was intended to be the Barclay rival for the redoubtable Johnny Halliday, who was, and most pundits say remains, the only major rock'n'roller that France has produced.

Eddy Mitchell did a lot of recording in London; at least eight EPs were made. For these recordings the session players were removed one step from their usual anonymity and retained a slightly altered moniker deriving from the album that Bobby had produced. They were called The London All Stars. They comprised Jimmy Page, Big Jim Sullivan and Bobby Graham. Others played on various tracks but this trio formed the recording core.

Other French artists who came to London and with whom Bobby recorded included Michel Polnareff, Eric Saint-Laurent and Sylvie Vartan. The one that made the greatest impression on Bobby, though, was Francoise Hardy. "She was simply lovely. She had a very warm and sexy voice and a beautiful personality. She spoke English with that wonderful French accent which had all the guys swooning over her. She was also very good at getting her own way; she would lapse into French pretending she didn't know what was going on and then smile sweetly when everyone capitulated. We made four EPs, three in French and one in English. So far as I am aware they did very well for her in France."

Bobby's role on the recording of Eddy Mitchell's first UK album *Eddy in London* was as a session drummer playing with the other Musical Stuntmen. They were under the direction of French musical director Jean Bouchety. Although it was the 'English Sound' that was sought to be replicated a French producer, Jean Fernandez, produced the album. Bobby and Jean rapidly established a rapport and found that they enjoyed each other's company.

One evening Jean Fernandez raised the possibility of Bobby moving to France to play drums for Eddy Mitchell who was very popular in his homeland and regularly played at the big stadiums. Bobby declined the offer saying that he saw his future in producing rather than session playing. In response to the inevitable supplementary question of who he was likely to be producing for, Bobby quickly invented an imminent meeting with Phillips Records. He said, they were interested in signing him on a permanent production contract.

Bobby remembers this conversation and was immediately uncomfortable with it. Whilst he was far from being a paragon of virtue during the decade, he had always tried to avoid lying about his own abilities, achievements or prospects. Others may disagree. More than one has commented on Bobby's ability to embellish a story to considerable effect. This, though, was different.

"I don't know what made me tell Jean what I did but, funnily enough, it seemed to have had the right effect."

Jean Fernandez response was immediate. He advised Bobby not to speak to Phillips until he had a chance to speak to "our guys." He went so far as to suggest that Bobby might wish to consider joining Disc Barclay as their international producer. He rang Bobby Graham later that night with the news that Eddie Barclay was flying from Paris for a breakfast meeting with Bobby at the Hilton Hotel in Park Lane.

Bobby's first meeting with Eddie Barclay has left an indelible impression that was confirmed by their every subsequent meeting. "He was a very elegant man in a very understated way; immaculate suits, he always wore a carnation in his buttonhole. He had a slim, pencil line moustache and it was obvious he liked the girls."

Eddie Barclay came straight to the point: "I would like to make you an offer." Whilst Bobby cannot remember the precise financial terms he knew straightaway that it was a fantastic offer. Some sixth sense told him that if he accepted too quickly he might be seen to be too compliant. He told Eddie Barclay that he would think about and when Eddie Barclay telephoned him later he began by saying "Bobby, if the money is not enough I will increase it". Bobby said that on those terms he would take the job: and so began his French Adventure.

His initial title was 'Managing Director Disc Barclay UK' although it was clear from the outset that the product of his work was principally for release on the French market.

Bobby's role was to scout for groups in the UK, produce and record them at the Pye Studios in London and then take the tapes to Paris were they would be released, almost always as EPs (extended play records) with four tracks. This format had been popular in the UK as a hybrid between the single with two tracks and the LP (longer player) that in the sixties almost always had twelve tracks. In France the EP format was extremely popular and there was a very willing audience. From the start Bobby's production was very successful and he became 'big in France' although without any great chart success. France was not such a great consumer of British pop music in the sense of record purchases but they listened to broadcast music a great deal.

However, in spite of this popularity, finding acts that would become popular in France was not easy. Bobby placed advertisements in the trade papers but the response was patchy. Those with talent and ambition did not wish to restrict their market potential. Those without talent were of no interest to Bobby.

A series of auditions were held in London and some talent emerged. The artists that Bobby recorded included The In-Betweens, some members of whom formed the backbone of Slade years later. He also recorded his old friend Bill Halsey with whom he had done the Butlins season as Billy Gray and The Stormers. They recorded an

EP with John Carter and Kenny Lewis singing backing vocals and with Jimmy Page on guitar. John Carter and Kenny Lewis were two of the most versatile and influential singers and songwriters of the sixties with a massive array of credits.

One EP that Bobby recalls with very mixed emotions was one of the first he recorded specifically to enthral the French. The EP was to be issued as 'Get Off My Cloud' by The Hairy Ones. Bobby assembled a brilliant ensemble of players, Jimmy Page on lead guitar, John McLoughlin on rhythm guitar, Alan Weighell on bass and Kenny Salmon on organ. It was decided that they would record four UK hits of the day. Firstly, 'Gloria' which had been the B side of Them's 'Baby Please Don't Go;' this had reached Number 10 in the charts earlier in 1965. Bobby had played on both sides of this recording. He, and posterity, think 'Gloria' was a better track than the A side.

The second track was to be 'It's My Life' which had reached Number 7 for The Animals in the autumn of the same year. Eric Burdon's strident and unique vocal style was a prominent feature of the track. This fact may not have been given the importance it deserved when choosing it for the EP. The third track, as the EP's title suggested was 'Get Off My Cloud' which was Number 1 in October 1965 for The Rolling Stones. The final track was a French sounding song entitled 'Ring Dang Do' which, unsurprisingly, was a hit for no-one.

The singer for the session was Ray Merrill a vocalist with The Joe Loss Band. Bobby is very anxious not to disparage Ray Merrill's vocal abilities although the context in which such singers operated is worthy of recollection.

"There were a number of orchestras who had regular radio slots, often lunch time midweek, things like *The Joe Loss Show* and some lunchtime listening where they were expected to play their standard repertoire but also the hits of the day. Singers were expected to be versatile: it was no good having a Ray Davies soundalike if he couldn't sing an Elvis Presley or a Cliff Richard number. So, a number of singers were used. Ray Merrill was one, Ross McManus another; they were versatile and could have a pretty good go at most things. Although in all truth you would rarely mistake their version for the original." Bobby says this with characteristic kindness and not a little understatement. Ray Merrill tried his best to tone down his BBC persona for the recording. "He did OK. But you have to listen to his Eric Burdon impersonation to believe it."

Another group that Bobby signed up and recorded were a Doncaster based group called The Staggerlees who took their name from the title of Lloyd Price's 1959 hit. The Staggerlees suffered a double ignominy; not one member of the group played on their own recording and the recording was probably never released. The recording was made by Bobby Graham, Jimmy Page, Eric Ford, Alan Weighell and Reg Guest on piano. Eric Ford played rhythm guitar on the session; he played six string bass on many sessions but was a much more accomplished rhythm player than anyone The Staggerlees could offer.

The job that Bobby had involved his flying to Paris, at least twice a week, to attend meetings; these were conducted entirely in French. There were many longer trips where he was accommodated at the best hotels. He spent a lot of time with Eddie Barclay. He was quick to criticise those that did not perform for him but even quicker to praise those that did. He was very happy with Bobby's work.

Although Bobby had moved within or just outside the circles of the highly successful for almost a decade, his exposure to Eddie Barclay's conspicuous success was illuminating and novel.

Two incidents brought home to Bobby the power and control of his employer and mentor. One evening after a long dinner, Bobby and his wife were told by Eddie Barclay that he was sending them to the South of France for a holiday because Bobby looked tired. He took out of his pocket a large wad of French francs and announced in French "Everybody to the gentlemen's lavatories." There Bobby and the others watched in amazement as he washed each note with soap and water before handing the sopping notes to Bobby. Eddie then made a comment which caused laughter amongst the French speakers and which Bobby asked the interpreter to translate: "He said he likes you so much and that you are such a nice guy and like a son but this is dirty money, he has made it in a bad way so he is washing it before he gives it to you." The holiday at Eddie Barclay's villa in Cannes was fantastic.

Eddie Barclay thrived on very little sleep; he enjoyed clubbing until the early hours and insisted that his friends and colleagues should accompany him. Bobby Graham was no slouch in this regard but even he occasionally found it too tiring. One evening Bobby declined a dinner invitation; this was not well received. Bobby used as his excuse his wish to see a film that was playing; it was *Dr Strangelove* starring Peter Sellers. Eddie Barclay seemed disappointed. A little later Eddie Barclay's secretary telephoned Bobby to say that Mr Barclay would like to go to the cinema, too. He would meet Bobby there at 7.00pm.

When Bobby arrived at the appointed time it was to be greeted by quite a large, clearly disaffected group of would-be cinema goers on the pavement. Jean Fernandez summoned Bobby inside to explain that Eddie had booked the whole cinema for his party.

Although the French never really took to the music that Disc Barclay UK produced, Bobby Graham had a great two years and produced some records that are memorable to him. His production skills were honed and he looks back on the time as a "highly paid production apprenticeship." But, the time came to move on and, not without many regrets, Bobby resigned his role and said "adieu" to Eddie Barclay.

Almost the Final Chapter

In the mid 1960s Bobby met a Dutch producer named Freddie Hayaan who was in London to record a band from the Netherlands called Golden Earring. Bobby was assigned to produce a recording of the group at the Pye Studios, London. Golden Earring were already a super group in Holland. During the session Bobby and Freddie chatted and exchanged phone numbers.

In 1968 news that Bobby had left Disc Barclay soon spread and it was not long before Freddie Hayaan contacted Bobby and invited him to the Netherlands to work for him, producing records for his company Red Bullet Productions. Bobby accepted the invitation and travelled to Hilversum. His time there proved to be short lived because he was soon sought by EMI who head hunted him to work for them in the Bovema recording studios in Heemstede, as executive international producer.

"I started producing Dutch artists for the international market. I got lucky; the first record I produced was for a group called Unit Gloria whose singer was a man named Robert Long."

The record was a major hit in the Netherlands and it gave Bobby a flying start. Robert Long went on to enjoy huge success not just in the Netherlands but elsewhere.

Bobby spent almost four years in Holland and produced a lot of very good records. But his time there passed in a haze, an alcoholic haze. His marriage to June had fallen apart and it was to be almost thirty years before he saw her or his daughter Tracy again.

"By 1971 my drinking had become horrendous and it was impossible to disguise it any more. Bovema asked me to leave and I found myself on the streets of Amsterdam full of booze, I don't think I realised I had a problem. I went from living a lavish lifestyle to living on the streets. It was almost the final chapter."

A Dutch/Indonesian family, the Van Heks, took pity on Bobby and looked after him until his parents learned of his plight and managed to get him back to the UK. Since then Bobby has never had another drink: he had, after all, had enough to last several lifetimes.

Epilogue

Bobby spent the early 1970s producing for Christian labels. He then opened a collectors' record shop in Edmonton but rapidly discovered that working nine until five was not for him. He has since enjoyed fifteen years success running a corporate video production company making videos for the Ladbroke Group, the Midland Bank and many other corporate organisations. He developed the skills of cameraman, editor and director. Unfortunately, his was one of many businesses that foundered in the recession of the late 1980s.

He was at a loss what to do. Then, one day, he saw a drum kit advertised for sale in a local newspaper.

"I thought I would buy it, clean it, set it up and sell it for a profit. I set it up in the front room and suddenly I was hooked again."

Bobby thought, probably inaccurately but with characteristic modesty, that no group would want an "old geezer however good he is" so he decided to start his own band, going back to his first love, jazz.

The Jazz Experience was formed and has enjoyed some considerable success, mostly in and around Hertfordshire. It is tempting to write more about this but it is not what this book is about. The very good news is that Bobby is living happily with his fourth wife Belinda and teenage son Shawn in Hertford. He spends much of his time visiting and lecturing at colleges and universities about his incredible musical journey. He is still playing the drums. His friend Hal Blaine gave Bobby some good advice: "Bobby we don't stop drumming because we get old, we get old because we stop drumming."

To those that ask "how well is Bobby playing these days?" then listen to his new CD *The Session Man* and you will find your answer.

There will probably never be another Bobby Graham. We should be thankful that there was one.

Acknowledgements

To my wife Belinda and son Shawn – thanks for loving me for what I am. Tracy, Harvey, Sam, Megan – my dear daughter and family. Ian Neate – they broke the mould when they made you, matey. Patrick and Susan Harrington – for making this all possible. Barry and Fe Green – for being good friends. Wendy Scott – one of my favourite characters for over 50 years now. Dave and Christine Smith – for your great support. Lol (the butler) – thanks mate for allowing me to continue playing. Mike, Helen, Cindy, Peter, Lizzie Caravello – our dear American family. With love and respect to you all.

And to Ray and Dave Davies, PJ Proby, Dave Berry, Mike Berry, Dave Clark, Englebert Humperdinck, Brian Poole, Jet Harris, Lulu, Petula Clark, Dusty Springfield, and the many, many others of talented people who helped stop my life from being one wasted, huge bore and made it into the most exciting journey any man could possibly travel.

Bobby Graham

To Susan for all of her help, her tolerance and under-standing. To the many people who have agreed to be interviewed, whether quoted in the book or not but especially Charles Blackwell, Billy Kuy, Big Jim Sullivan, Mike Berry, Dave Berry, Joe Brown, Marty Wilde, PJ Proby, John Morris, Ray Davies, Dave Davies, Mike D'Abo, John Carter, Stan Barrett, John Reptch, Shel Talmy, Dick Taylor, Phil May, Andy Butler, John Briggs and Geoff Nicholls. Also David Potter, Simon Schwarz and John Bowen who kept me going when the pressure was on.

Patrick Harrington

The author

Patrick Harrington is a QC practising from chambers in London. He is a former Leader of the Wales and Chester Circuit and specialises in criminal law.

As a teenager in the South Wales Valleys he played guitar in a number of groups, sharing billing with Tommy Scott (Tom Jones), Wayne Fontana and the Mindbenders and Andy Fairweather Low amongst others. In 1986 he was inspirational in forming the all-barrister band Brief Encounter in which he played bass guitar (very badly). He is a child of the sixties and remains hooked on the music of the time. He lives with his wife Susan in Raglan. They have a daughter and a son.

Index

Index

Index